through art we care

2

Preface

It is hard to pinpoint exactly when the story began that led to the book you are now holding in your hands. Perhaps we should go back to 1997, with the opening of the palliative and supportive day care centre TOPAZ by the Vrije Universiteit Brussel. TOPAZ seeks to offer a warm home to anyone who is confronted with a serious, incurable condition. From its earliest days, guests (as patients are called) not only receive medical, paramedical and psychosocial care at TOPAZ, but can also participate in creative, recreational and artistic workshops, provided by volunteers and creative and artistic therapists. In other words, a certain openness towards art has always been part of the centre's DNA. However, inviting professional artists to work as artists in residence at TOPAZ—which was the IN/FINITY project's aim—was still a different story altogether. It was the enthusiasm and commitment of some key figures that gave TOPAZ the confidence to be that ambitious. Through personal encounters, ideas crystallised into a concrete project. From an international perspective, the 'London Lighthouse' was an important source of inspiration. This famous care centre for people with HIV and AIDS, which opened in Notting Hill (London) in 1988 was deeply linked to the art world, which was hit hard by the AIDS crisis. One important aim of the IN/FINITY project was to investigate and make explicit the artistic heritage of this generation of artists. Faced with loss and finiteness but also care, these artists often addressed these themes in their work. These topics are equally relevant for our time, in which death is often considered a taboo subject, while, thanks to ideas such as 'transhumanism', there is a new optimism surrounding the pursuit of immortality. All the while, the concept of 'care' seems to be under pressure in all sections of our society. Enough starting points for an artistic research project on the intersection between arts and palliative and supportive care.

IN/FINITY could only really come into being thanks to the generous support of the Flemish Minister of Art and Culture Sven Gatz and a project subsidy from the Flemish Kunstendecreet. This support allowed TOPAZ to invite several professional artists over a period of three years to realise an artistic trajectory at TOPAZ, based on an ongoing dialogue with the centre and its guests. TOPAZ' name is a reference to the gemstone with multiple intersections that symbolises openness and respect for others, regardless of their skin colour, origin, sexual orientation or social status. The centre received the artists with the same welcoming attitude with which it approaches its guests. No 'musts' or 'don'ts', but openness, curiosity and tolerance towards every individual and what they may bring: it's a philosophy that fits very well with the credo of the contemporary art world and proved to offer a safe and fertile context for the artists involved.

Christian Bakalov, Naomi Kerkhove, Emi Kodama, Jorge León, Rudi Meulemans, ORACLE (Michel Yang, Justine Maxelon and Caroline Daish), Michael Schmid and Vera Tussing were the artists selected, based on qualities in their artistic work that seemed to hold a promise for a rich dialogue with TOPAZ and its guests. They are active in various media: literature, dance, theatre, visual arts, performance, music, etc., and differ greatly in terms of their artistic profile and interests. Their IN/FINITY trajectories are equally divergent. What they share is that they don't approach the guests of TOPAZ as 'material' or 'resources' for an artistic end product but as equal partners in a dialogue. These relationships themselves often became the artistic material and theme of their work. Sometimes, the artistic medium—whether drawing, music, movement or touch—functioned as catalyst, sometimes as facilitator for an encounter. It could shape the dialogue, scan the limits of coexistence or function as 'residue': a tangible trace of shared moments. When artists did realise an artistic 'product', it was primarily understood as just one pearl in a string of encounters, an experience that could inspire the ongoing conversation.

The result was a small-scale and ephemeral way of working that—while experienced as very rich and meaningful by those closely involved—hardly allowed the external viewer a glimpse inside. This is what we hope to offer, to a certain extent, through this book. You will find contributions from not only the artists involved in IN/FINITY but also from like-minded artists, experts and organisations in whom we found inspiring discussion partners. IN/FINITY arose from personal encounters, and it was through personal encounters that it grew organically, ultimately far beyond the context of TOPAZ. We hope that this book reflects its spirit of dialogue by juxtaposing different voices and stories in different chapters, each focusing on a theme that surfaced throughout the process of IN/FINITY. Above all, the contributions ask for a dialogue with you, implicitly or explicitly, by offering you instructions that you can perform, giving you an embodied idea of the proposals that the artists formulated for the TOPAZ guests. This book is not intended as a final word, but rather as a snapshot, which will hopefully inspire more dialogues, exchanges and initiatives. It should not be considered as a manual, providing a ready-made method for those who wish to connect art, palliative care and healthcare. If IN/FINITY has taught us anything, it is that such collaborations cannot be designed according to a fixed methodology. The best way to navigate this domain is not with the help of a roadmap, having a predetermined goal in mind, but with a compass at hand: willing to constantly reorient and question yourself from where you are at any given moment. It requires curiosity, generosity and courage, which everyone involved has shown in abundance. It has created this diverse, intricate and infinite patchwork of ideas, images, moments and memories that may now live on.

Wouter Bouchez & Julie Rodeyns,
Curators/Mediators IN/FINITY
Frank Schweitser,
Head Nurse TOPAZ
Wim Distelmans,
Initiator and Director TOPAZ
Free De Backer,
Professor Educational Sciences Vrije Universiteit Brussel
Marc Noppen,
CEO Universitair Ziekenhuis Brussel
Caroline Pauwels,
Rector Vrije Universiteit Brussel

7

8

IN... BETWEEN

9

In the whole process of bridging art and health paradigms, there is an important role for the mediator. This person who, on one hand, has both extensive knowledge of the arts world and of art in general, and on the other hand also understands the functioning and challenges of the healthcare sector, is often a key player in successful art and health projects. In the first place, this mediator must be a good listener and translator of ideas. Misconceptions and bad communication are always the biggest but also one the most common pitfalls in art-health collaborations.

We invited Anna Ledgard (UK), Jérome Poggi (FR) and Julie Rodeyns (BE), all three of them professional mediators with experience in art-health collaborations, to talk about their role, projects and their lessons learnt.

Not of Use but of Value, the Art Curator as Mediator in Art-Health Collaborations

Julie Rodeyns

10

The word 'curator' comes from the Latin 'curare', which means 'to care for'. One could say that an art curator cares for art objects in a museum space. In a broader sense, their object of concern is not only the physical aspect of the artworks, but also their mental meaning: their content and its social and cultural implications. What can art do in society? Curators increasingly look to answer this question outside the walls of the 'black box' of the theatre or the 'white cube' of the gallery space. They position themselves as a 'mediator', creating meaningful encounters between art and other domains in society. It is this role that my colleague Wouter Bouchez and I took on in the IN/FINITY project. I travelled to Paris and London, where I respectively met fellow art professionals Jérôme Poggi and Anna Ledgard, curious to learn how they understand their role as art curator/mediator in specifically art-health collaborations.

A. THE ART CURATOR AS MEDIATOR

'Connecting different people and practices and causing the conditions for triggering sparks between them', is how famous curator Hans Ulrich Obrist defines the practice of an art curator. 'Sparks' arise when you approach your discussion partner not as a customer or a pupil, but as an equal party, who can learn from you but from whom you can also learn. This is where the work of an art curator as mediator differs from that of an art educator or marketeer. In our compartmentalised society, where different knowledge worlds operate independently from each other—each with its own philosophy, truths, values, specific language and objectives—an encounter between different worlds (for instance art and health) can quite literally generate fireworks. At worst, this can lead to misunderstandings, prejudices, resistance, polarisation, or at its most extreme, the appropriation of one domain by the other, the appropriating domain imposing its laws and logic onto the appropriated. It is perhaps the most challenging and important responsibility of the curator as mediator to guard against this. To instil a culture of genuine dialogue, curiosity, mutual interest and trust between all parties and actors involved requires caring guidance and, above all, time. Once achieved, it can provide fertile soil for a truly explorative collaboration.

Here, the curator as mediator morphs into the role of guide: leading all into unfamiliar territory, as these newly established relationships can cause new meaning and ideas to develop, which can potentially transform all parties involved. Thus, when the palliative and supportive day care centre TOPAZ (Belgium) approached my colleague curator/mediator Wouter Bouchez and myself, articulating a desire to invite professional artists to work with their guests (as they call the patients) at their facility, we had no idea where this would take us. Nonetheless, we felt confident that this idea could generate something meaningful.

Both art and health hold 'care' as their core value. They share a long history of mutual interest, at times even blending together. During the Middle Ages, for instance, art was understood to be part of the repertoire of remedies a doctor had at hand. Since Modernity, the two domains have become alienated from one another. In medicine, new developments and technologies led away from a holistic pursuit of health towards a biomedical approach. The patient was reduced to a physical body, a doctor now treats dysfunctional body parts. Social, psychological or behavioural factors are not much taken into account. From the perspective of art, ever since the motto of 'art for art's sake' was articulated in the 19th century, the idea that art shouldn't have any goal became fundamental to the concept of art. To date, the art world still largely retains this idea. However, the past two decades have seen art and health beginning to share a story again. In the current neoliberal climate, in both domains the core value of 'care' is under pressure, a matter that seemed urgent enough to Wouter Bouchez and myself to make us curious to explore what new ideas an encounter between these two worlds could generate.

B. WHEN ART IS NOT AN OPTION

Such an exploration is miles away from the goal of improving the health and well-being of patients through art, an idea that has gained immense popularity thanks to art and creative therapies. With its roots in psychoanalysis, art therapy is, however, first and foremost a clinical practice, highly regulated by specific guidelines and a professional code of ethics. Therefore, there is no role for art curators/mediators in art-health collaborations that are situated in the realm of art therapy. Conversely, one cannot expect a professional artist to do what an art therapist does: making patients better. My conversation partners point out two other situations where engaging a professional artist might not be the right answer. 'If you have a merely decorative need, you should engage a designer and not a professional artist,' says Jérôme Poggi. He talks vividly about his initial meetings with the clinicians of the palliative care unit of Groupe Hospitalier Diaconesses Croix Saint-Simon in Paris. When they expressed their wish to commission a work of art, at first the curator had had his reservations: 'I told them that if they wanted something to brighten up their corridors, they might better go to the museum shops of the Centre Pompidou or Musée d'Orsay and buy some Monet or Van Gogh posters.' It was only when they told Poggi that they had already put up art posters and also paid special attention to the decoration of the spaces, choosing colourful walls and appropriate furniture, that the curator grew convinced that he could mean something to them. 'It became clear that, although they had tried everything in their power and knowledge to answer a need for art, they didn't know how to answer or even put it in words, as they aren't art experts. There was clearly a very strong desire, as they had already gone to all these efforts and expenses and still wanted something different, something more.' Anna Ledgard mentions another common misconception about art and health collaborations, namely when the artist is seen as a messenger for the health professional. Ledgard:

'This idea that art can help to draw attention to medical problems and educate the audience, that's not what we're about either.' She takes a recent project by artist Sofie Layton as an example. Her exhibition 'The Heart of the Matter' (London, 2018), for which she closely collaborated with biomedical engineer Giovanni Biglino, was inspired by encounters and collaborations with patients with heart conditions and their families. Ledgard: 'Yes, we would be delighted if people see this exhibition and go away thinking more carefully about their heart. However, it might be our intention to provoke thought about the importance of our hearts and bodies, but it is not our intention to educate people to go jogging five times a day, which would actually be inappropriate as we were working with people with inherited heart conditions who could do nothing about their condition.'

C.
EXPLORING OPTIONS FOR ART

Whereas my colleagues are very outspoken about the circumstances in which art is not an option, they are much more cautious and nuanced when I ask them when art can be an option. We enter murky waters where boundaries cannot always be drawn clearly. Anna Ledgard starts by pointing out that techniques that professional artists work with are not necessarily dissimilar from techniques that art therapists use. Ledgard: 'When working with chronically ill children, theatre maker Mark Storor used metaphoric associative exercises to start up the creative process. It gives people the liberty and possibility to talk about things that they may have difficulty talking about.' The conversations eventually led to a theatre performance, shown in public theatres: 'For the Best' (2009). According to Ledgard, this sets Storor's work apart from art therapy: 'our work may start with an individual conversation but is then shared: first with other people in the same position in order to become a collective expression and then, usually, with a wider audience.'

At first glance, Ledgard's statement may seem to contradict the choices Wouter Bouchez and I made with IN/FINITY. In the context of a palliative and supportive day care centre, reaching a collective expression did not prove to be either achievable or desirable, and neither was the idea of exposing the guests to the gaze of others. When, for example, artist/writer Rudi Meulemans invited the guests for a day at the seaside, the guests were warmly welcomed by the art festival that hosted us, but the event was—at our request—not mentioned anywhere in the festival brochure. That day, the guests of TOPAZ were first and foremost festival guests among other festival guests, reconnected with this realm of society that they often feel excluded from. This very fragile situation would be broken if too much emphasis was placed on their presence and specific condition, as this would again set them apart. A few days later, the text that Rudi Meulemans had written especially for that day at the seaside and for the guests appeared in a national newspaper. The link between the text and the ambiance of that unique, quite glorious day may be lost on its readers.

Yet, the guests were in the know (and the newspaper clipping received a central place on the TOPAZ bulletin board). Perhaps more indirectly than in the example of Marc Storor's theatre performance mentioned by Anna Ledgard, nonetheless, through the text written by Rudi Meulemans (as well as other IN/FINITY actions and interventions by the other artists involved), the guests of TOPAZ too, in a way, enter into a dialogue with a wider audience.

In other words: the notion of creating connections with society at large is not only central to Anna Ledgard's story but also to our story and, quite remarkably, also, though with other nuances, to the story of Jérôme Poggi, who works with the staff of the palliative care unit of the Groupe Hospitalier Diaconesses Croix Saint-Simon. During an early visit to the department, Poggi noticed that every room had a tear-off calendar. Poggi: 'The doctors explained to me that, for them, it was really important to consider their patients as members of society and thus as connected with the time of our society, the time we all share. In a hospital, you easily lose track of time, hence the calendar. The intention was good, but they didn't find the right form, which is exactly where an artist can play a key role.' The commission was entrusted to artist Mathieu Lehanneur, who conceived a high-tech installation for each room: a round screen—hardly noticeable in the general setting—that shows tomorrow's sky, 24 hours from now. Poggi: 'The patient can use a remote control to choose what sky is shown: the sky over Paris or any other place, for instance somewhere they have family. Of course, it's a highly symbolic work: showing us the time that we will share tomorrow and the place where we'll all go, eventually. At the same time, the object also functions as conversation starter. Often when you enter a hospital room, you don't know what to talk about and you end up talking about the weather—a word that in French is the same word as for time.' The artwork has had a remarkable side-effect. Lehanneur created one installation to show in the art circuit. It was on display in many exhibitions. Its image became very popular and popped up in various media to accompany articles on death and grieving, instead of more traditional images of a person walking through an open door. Again, a conversation in small circle led to a new idea that inspired society, in this case, changing the visual image of a certain topic. A talented and sensitive art curator/mediator should not only see when art is an option, but also how a work of art can resonate beyond the specific context for which it has been envisioned.

D.
WHAT ART MEDIATORS DO

It is already clear that the work of an art curator/mediator encompasses much more than 'finding money': an idea that people often seem to hold at the start, Ledgard tells me. 'I do raise money, but that's only a very small part of what I do.' Her starting point is different from how Jérôme Poggi, Wouter Bouchez and I work, in the sense that she always works with the same small group of artists. The initiative for a collaboration can come from one of them as well as from a healthcare partner. Jérôme Poggi, Wouter Bouchez and I always work on behalf of a social partner. As members of 'New Patrons', both Jérôme Poggi and I follow the protocol developed by this international network of curators/mediators, but in the end, our approach is not that different from how Ledgard and Bouchez work. Conversation is key. Through careful listening, we envision what art could mean for a specific question that the healthcare partner holds. Then, based on our expertise and knowledge of the contemporary art world, we select (an) artist(s) who could answer this question. Not every artist is suitable for every commission, but previous experience in healthcare is not necessarily required, Ledgard, Poggi, Bouchez and I agree. What's more important is the intuition you have as curator/mediator that this coming together of different actors may generate something meaningful. It demands a leap of faith, but at the same time requires vigilance. Ledgard: 'You have to be very careful, as there might be something very exciting for artists to gain access to such situations. This can't be their motivation. We are in a position of extraordinary responsibility. We may not be dealing with the medical side of the body, but we are dealing with feelings and minds!' In the end, trust is key, in all directions. The artist has to trust the curator to not only respect their artistic integrity, but also to know that there is space for their art to be present in the first place. In some medical contexts, an artistic gesture may feel futile or—at the other extreme—too heavy a responsibility. Poggi: 'When I first approached Matthieu Lehanneur about this commission, he found it very challenging. He asked me if I realized that I was asking him to imagine an object that might be the last thing that dying people will see.' Finally, the healthcare partner also needs to respect the expertise of the art curator/mediator, which might pose the biggest challenge. All of my conversation partners are familiar with the DIY mentality of the sometimes overly self-confident medical world. We all agree on this: the medical world should understand that the art world is very specific, and that expertise, cues and keys are needed. It's a message that is under huge pressure in our society where, on the one hand, it's quite fashionable to call yourself 'professional artist', even when you lack the skills, education or recognition (which renders the notion of 'professional artist' quite meaningless) and where, on the other hand, art is increasingly expected to have a demonstrable social relevance. How, in such a climate, can we defend our position: to strive—instead of taking a merely utilitarian approach—to combine a genuine dialogue between art and healthcare professionals with a high-quality artistic end result, without compromising either? It's Jérôme Poggi who, through an anecdote about the funding of Lehanneur's project, provides me with an answer. Poggi: 'With its high-tech components, Matthieu Lehanneur's work was quite expensive. When I asked the head of department how he planned to justify this to his colleagues at the hospital, he replied that their department works differently from other departments. While other services want to dismiss people as quickly as possible, he likes to keep them as long as possible. He told me that a work of art may have no use, just as an extra day to live may have no use, but it may be of value.' That which is, perhaps, not of use but of value: it's quite a good summary of what we stand for.

Many thanks to: Wouter Bouchez, Free De Backer, Anna Ledgard, Thérèse Legierse, Jérôme Poggi.

17

18

19

20

21

22

23

24

THE SENSES AS TRIGGERS OF THE SOUL

The French say: 'une caresse pour les yeux/les oreilles' (a caressing of one's eyes or ears) upon seeing or hearing something beautiful. Our senses have a very direct link with our emotions, our feelings and, by extension, our well-being. More than anyone else, artists are masters of the senses, so it's not very surprising to see that many artists in an art and health context feel a strong desire to explore this notion of sensoriality and the ways in which sensory manipulation, stimulation and deprivation affect our well-being, our awareness, our feelings and our bodies.

Christian Bakalov's work aims to create an immersive context where the sensory experience—the visual, auditive and tactile—is central. Borrowing ideas from the performing arts, wellness practices and new age philosophies, among others, he takes his audience members on both a physical and emotional journey to an alternate universe.

Body Sensing Routine
Christian Bakalov

26

‘Body Sensing Routine’ introduces you to a series of simple exercises that reconnect your body awareness with your direct experience. This routine explores intimacy and tactility, introducing us to a total experience in which the physical, emotional and symbolic body is moved, affected and transformed.

(1)

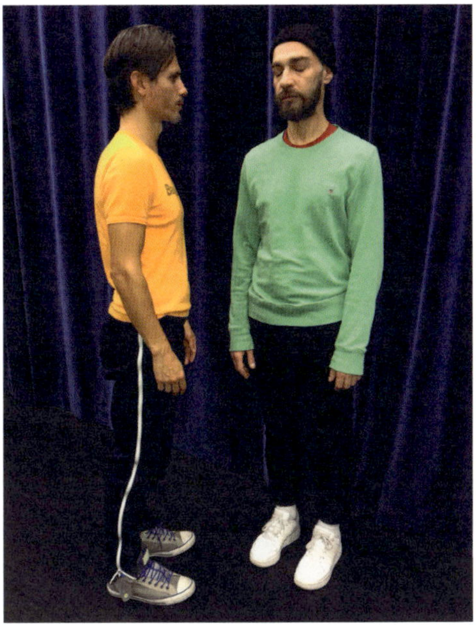

‘Body Sensing’ can be performed with your partner standing or sitting, depending on his or her physical condition. The session starts by asking your partner to close his or her eyes and to concentrate on their breathing. Wait 1 minute to let your partner find the rhythm of his/her breathing. During this time, warm your hands by rubbing them together. Once your hands are really warm, starting with your fingertips, gently place the palm of your hand in the middle of your partner’s chest. For this first contact and all that follows, it’s very important that your hand doesn’t apply any pressure to your partner’s body. It’s important to imagine your hands as a connector through which energy can flow between both of your bodies. The contact between you and your partner has to be as pure as possible and should not be transmitting any emotional or psychological intention. The only aim of the contact that matters is to allow the two bodies to connect to each other and regulate themselves.

(2)

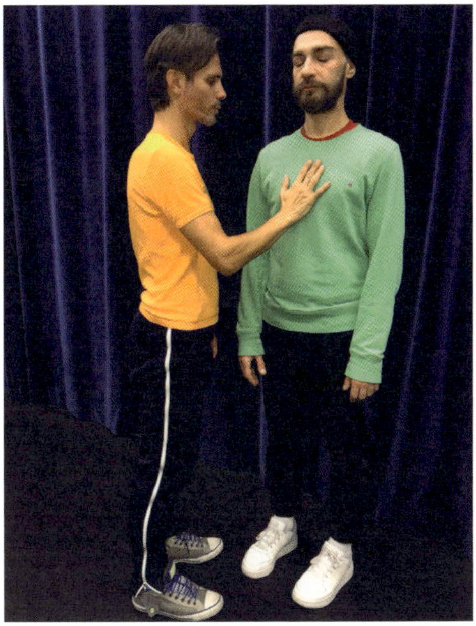

The first contact always starts on the chest/sternum. Once your hand is fully on your partner’s chest, slowly count to 5, which is approximately 10 seconds.

(3)

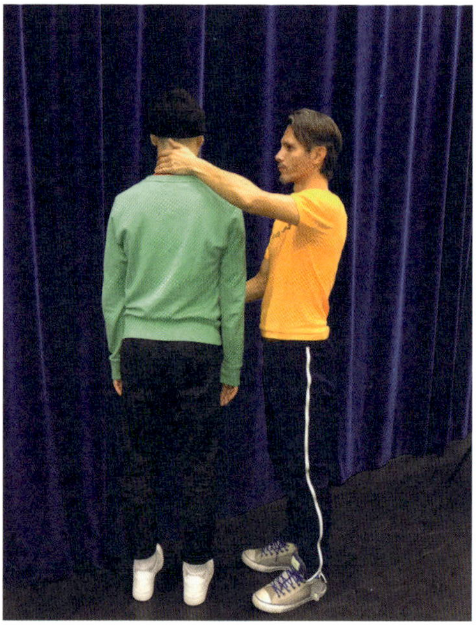

Once you've finished counting to 5, initiate the second contact by placing your left hand on your partner's neck. In this gesture, it's important that your thumb stays connected to the other fingers, and that you don't grab the neck as you would grab a glass of water.

(4)

You are now in contact with your partner through your two hands: one on the chest and the other on the neck. Start counting slowly to 5 again. Once you've finished, slowly remove your first hand from the chest, and move your hand to your partner's cheek, leaving it there for 10 seconds (or counting slowly to 5).

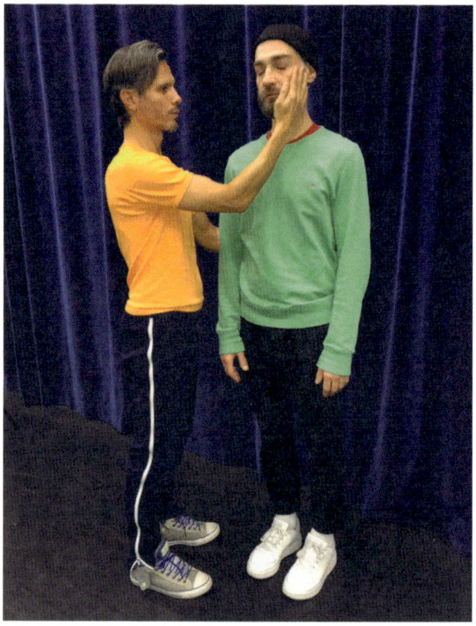

(5)

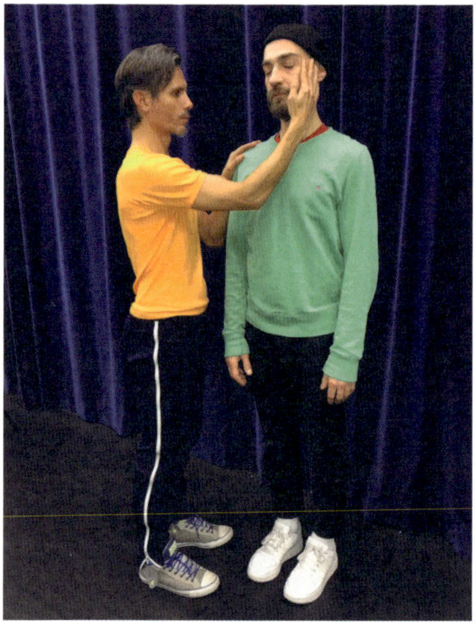

After that, your hand that is on the neck moves down to your partner's shoulder and stays there for 10 seconds.

(6)

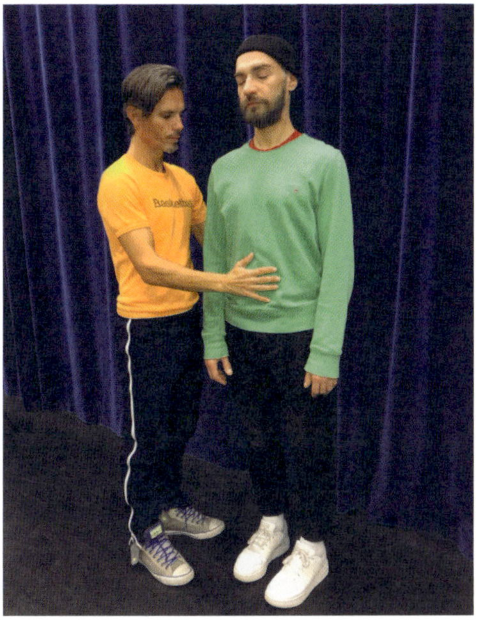

Your right hand goes from the cheek onto the belly of your partner and stays there for 10 seconds.

(7)

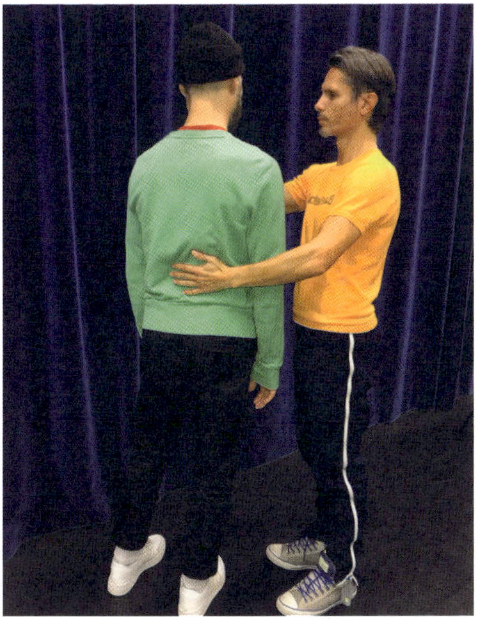

Your left hand moves from your partner's shoulder to his/her lower back and stays there for 10 seconds. In this position, you can mentally connect both of your hands by imagining the energy flowing between them.

(8)

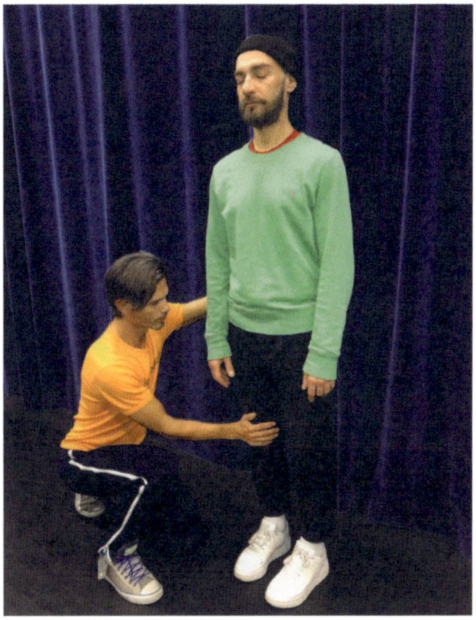

Your right hand moves to your partner's knee for 10 seconds.

(9)

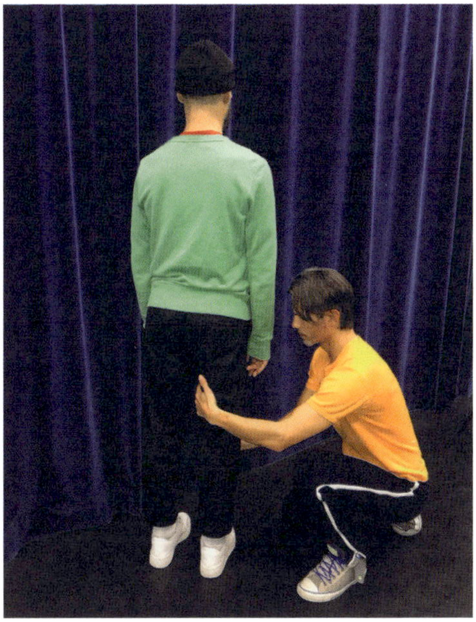

Your left hand moves to your partner's inner thigh (reach from behind) and stays there for 10 seconds.

(10)

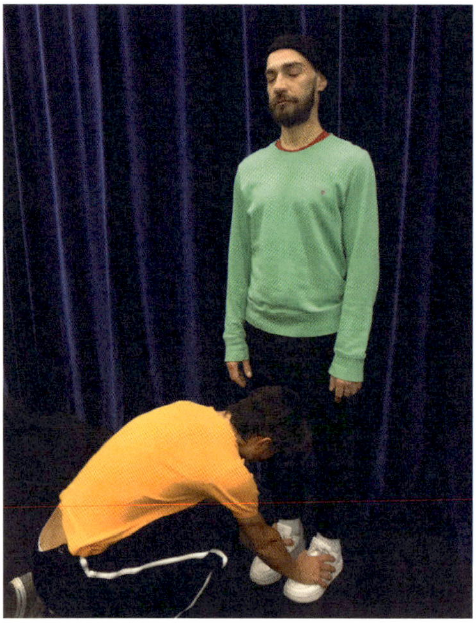

After that, place both your hands on your partner's two feet and push them into the floor to 'ground' your partner. This is the only moment that you can apply some more pressure to your partner's body. Stay here, 'grounding' your partner, for 20 seconds.

(11, 12, 13)

Next, gently take your partner's wrists in your hands. By standing up slowly, start bringing your partner's arms up sideways, all the way until they are above his or her head. The movement of the two arms is synchronised and very slow. It will take between 50 seconds and 1 minute to bring them up, depending on the weight of your partner's arms. Only hold the wrists, leaving your partner's hands free to move.

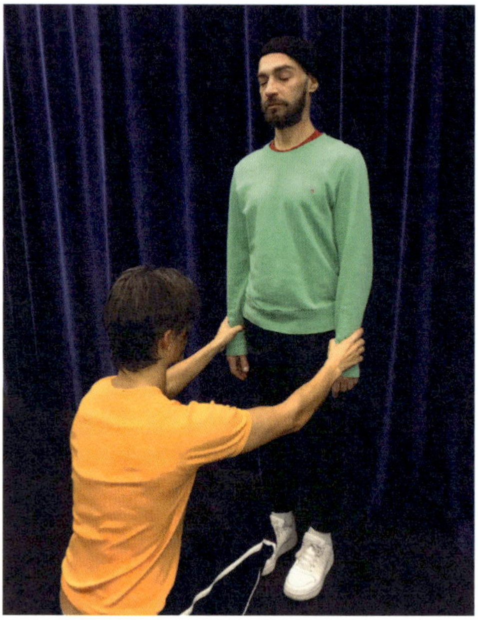

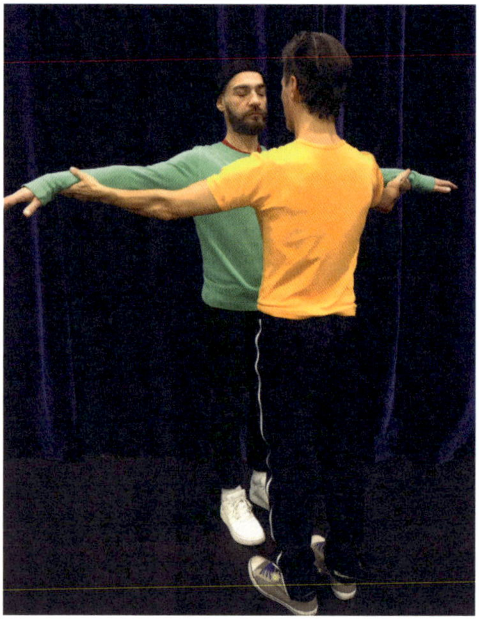

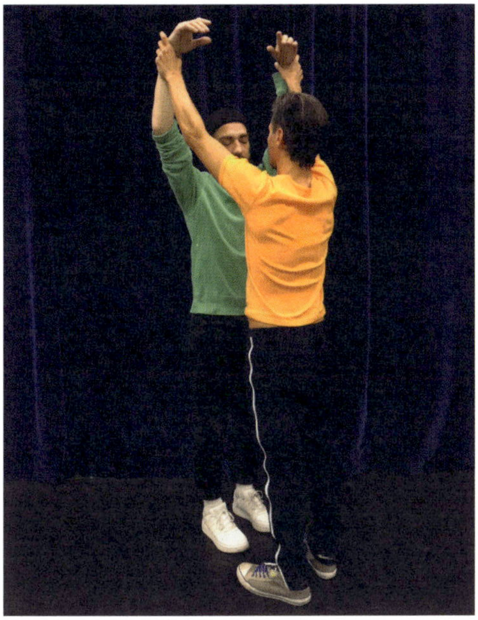

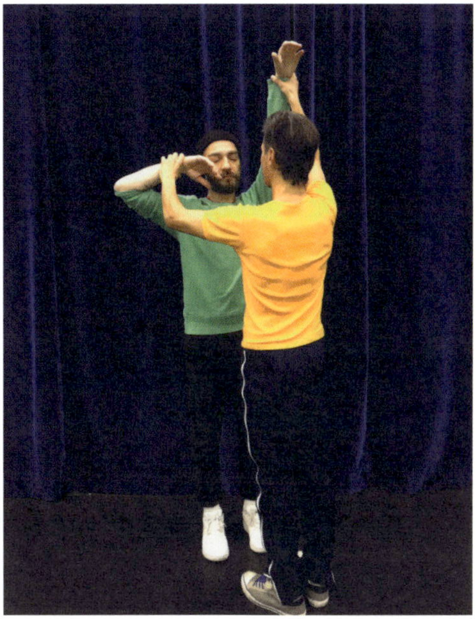

(14, 15)
Once both arms are up above the head, desynchronise them and start to move them in any direction you want, separately, but always at the same speed and without any acceleration.

Keep your partner's two arms moving continually (but never force them backwards). They can be bent and crossed in front of your partner's body. Feel free to explore the space around with your partner's arms for a few minutes.

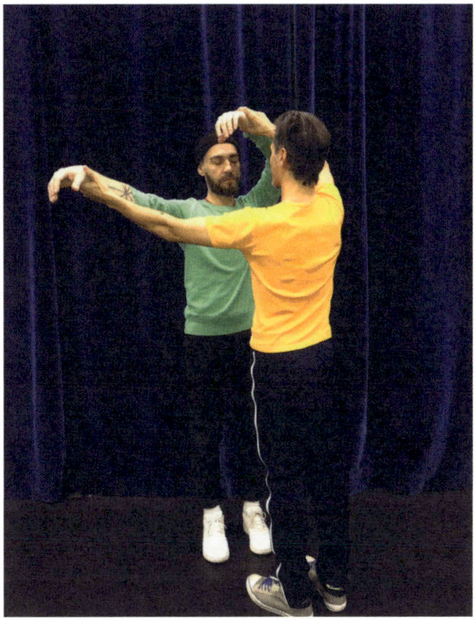

The only touches you have to perform on your partner while moving the arms are with his or her own hands. First, make your partner's hand caress his/her cheek, from bottom to top. Second, using the other hand, stroke his/her forehead from one side to the other. During these manipulations, it's very important that you only hold the wrist and not the hand itself, so that the hands are free to move and are able to caress and stroke the face. This part can last between 3-5 minutes, depending how receptive your partner is.

(16)

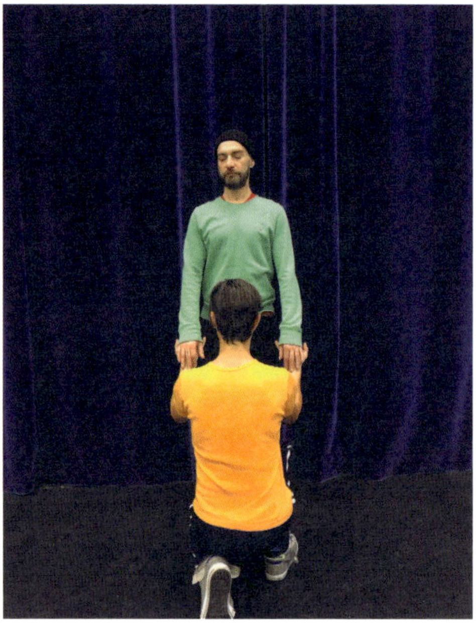

Once you finish this part, you bring your partner's two arms above his/her head and let them come down very slowly (1 minute), but this time let them pass in front of the body until you return to the starting position.

(17)

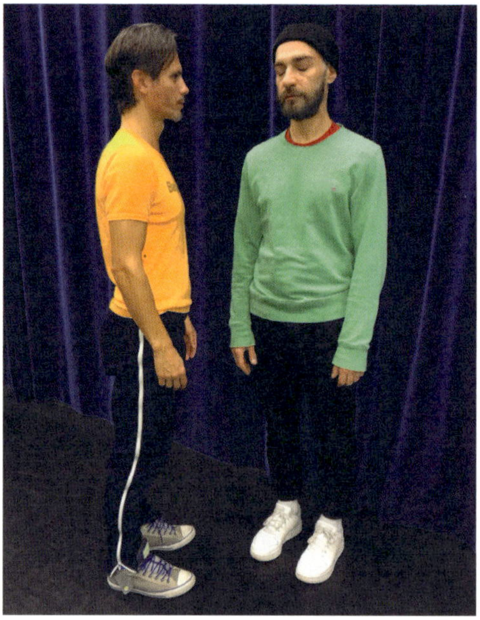

Very slowly, take your hands off your partner's body.

— End of Body Sensing

While performing 'Body Sensing', it is very important to keep the speed of the movement very slow and to avoid accelerating your movements.

Never force the movement of your partner's arms. If you feel resistance, gently 'shake' them to encourage your partner to drop control of their movement.

'Body sensing' can be performed by one to five performers on one person. In the case of more than one performer, we recommend the person undergoing 'Body Sensing' to lay on the floor, so that each performer can move an arm or a leg each.

During 'Body Sensing', the eyes of the subject are always closed.

Enjoy and never forget that we are all one.

33

34

35

36

38

39

40

SPACE FOR CARING

Our healthcare system often seems to confuse caring with curing. In a society that is so focused on well-being, our care facilities are usually organised and designed in a way that may be optimal for curing, but not for providing a welcoming social space that appeals to its users, a space that makes them feel good (or even better). The more artists we met who work within a healthcare context, and the more they talked with patients and healthcare professionals, the more we noticed a desire among these artists to address the idea of space. Not only physical space, but also mental, emotional, creative and social space. Caring and curing is as much related to the body as it is to the mind. Creating such an open and welcoming space for caring seemed to be necessary as the basis and catalyst for many successful art and health projects.

Over the next couple of pages, we would like to introduce you to 'Madlove: an ideal asylum', a workshop project by Hannah Hull and James Leadbitter aka the vacuum cleaner, two artists who apply a creative and collective approach to explore this notion of a multi-layered and multi-dimensional space for caring.

Art is a world where much is possible, where the concerns are not the same as elsewhere. In general, there is more freedom and less uniformity, there are fewer rules and fewer social constraints. One can afford a lot more here than elsewhere. Many examples of provocative art bear witness to this freedom. There is no sexual, religious or political taboo that has not been broken by artists. Moreover, within the arts, there is more tolerance towards people who colour outside the lines, which makes it a good place for them to dwell.

Considering the many links and overlaps between art and psychological vulnerability, more could be done to create synergies between the fields of art and psychiatric care. With KAOS, we aim to contribute to such synergies. KAOS is an acronym for KunstAtelier OpperStraat. It refers to the street on which we're located, but also to the birthplace of the Italian playwright, novelist, and short-story writer Luigi Pirandello (1867- 1936) and the beautiful '84 film by the Taviani brothers, based on Pirandello's short stories. Of course, it also refers to chaos, the divergent outlook on things. We support art projects that have a certain link with psychiatry, but which put artistic quality first. KAOS is a space where, by establishing these unique connections, we seek to counteract the distinction between insiders and outsiders made in the art world and in society at large. This is our credo in a nutshell. Since 2011, we have been organising exhibitions, performances and concerts, and have successfully introduced artists with a mental health condition to the regular art world. We also often collaborate with other players in the art field, as the idea of connecting and reaching out is fundamental to our work. The cornerstone of the KAOS project, however, is our artist residency in psychiatry. We invite artists to stay, live and work in a sheltered housing project. We ask them to develop an artistic project with the patients, culminating in an exhibition, a performance and/or a publication. This wording is inadequate, as we believe that at KAOS, 'artist' and 'patient' are interchangeable concepts. This is not just wishful thinking: our experience shows that the residency is essentially a meeting and exchange between people who quickly come to see one another as friends and colleagues, creating a common creative space.

In February 2018, we invited Hannah Hull and James Leadbitter, aka 'the vacuum cleaner' to bring their workshop 'Madlove—a designer asylum' to KAOS, a project that fit very nicely in this context. Their approach to engaging the patients in an artistic dialogue around the spaces in which psychiatric care takes place is critical, refreshing, constructive and simply very important. As a psychiatrist responsible for the care provided in the small psychiatric facility where KAOS was born, I benefited from all the ideas generated by the 'Madlove' workshop to improve our care provision. The workshop took place in the KAOS atelier, and I participated in a somewhat distinctive way. As I was assigned the task of illustrating the workshop's ideas, I did not contribute to the debate. Instead, I listened attentively to everything that was said and tried to turn the many ideas into images. This proved to be another link between art and psychiatry: patients and artists creating the physical, social and mental space of psychiatric care. While drawing as fast as I could, because ideas were flowing very quickly, I noticed that some ideas were easily imaginable. These are ideas linked to the physical circumstances of psychiatric care. They include proposals about nice spaces with many possibilities and original activities, and they shared a remarkable focus on sensorial enjoyment: spaces and surroundings that are pleasurable to the eye and the ear, but also nice to smell, touch and taste. This may seem self-evident, but unfortunately, it is in stark contrast with psychiatric architectural reality in many places. Psychiatric and other healthcare facilities with nicknames such as 'the bathroom', 'the boot camp' and 'the morgue' say it all. Many of the ideas generated in the workshop came close to what anyone would imagine, not about an ideal hospital but about an ideal home, which is an important message. To hear these ideas expressed so clearly was enriching, to say the least. Other ideas arising in the course of the workshop were much more difficult to turn into images, because they dealt with invisible, personal and essential qualities of the caregiving process. Participants held that this process should be open, caring, warm, joyful, not controlling, beautiful, curious, reflective, optimistic, etc. Once again, these are not qualities that we think of when we envision the ideal psychiatric professional, but qualities that we enjoy in friends and family, another important message to take home.

After hearing these ideas arising in the workshop, I had to think of Archimedes, who made a great discovery in his bath, whereupon he ran naked through the streets shouting 'Eureka'. A wonderful example of how daydreaming, musing and associative wandering through your mind can lead to new insights and can go hand in hand with strange behaviour. It is age-old folk wisdom that artists are at least somewhat eccentric, that the heads of poets and philosophers are always in the clouds, and scientists are often distracted and sometimes simply mad. The distance that separates art and psychiatry is a small one, and sometimes, the two worlds overlap. The creative process has a lot to do with a way of thinking that encompasses musing, daydreaming, fantasising, mind-wandering and breaking with traditions while dealing with the unknown. I call this state of mind 'fruitful and fragile'. Nothing embodies this better than 'Madlove', which guides us from this mindset to 'fruitful and fragile places': a refreshing new common space for health- and psychiatric care. May we continue to wonder...

Illustrations:
'Madlove — a designer asylum'
Workshops drawn by:
Erik Thys (p.45, 48, 49, 52-55),
Michael Duckett (p.46, 47),
Lewis Campbell — LostMonkey Art
(p.50-51)

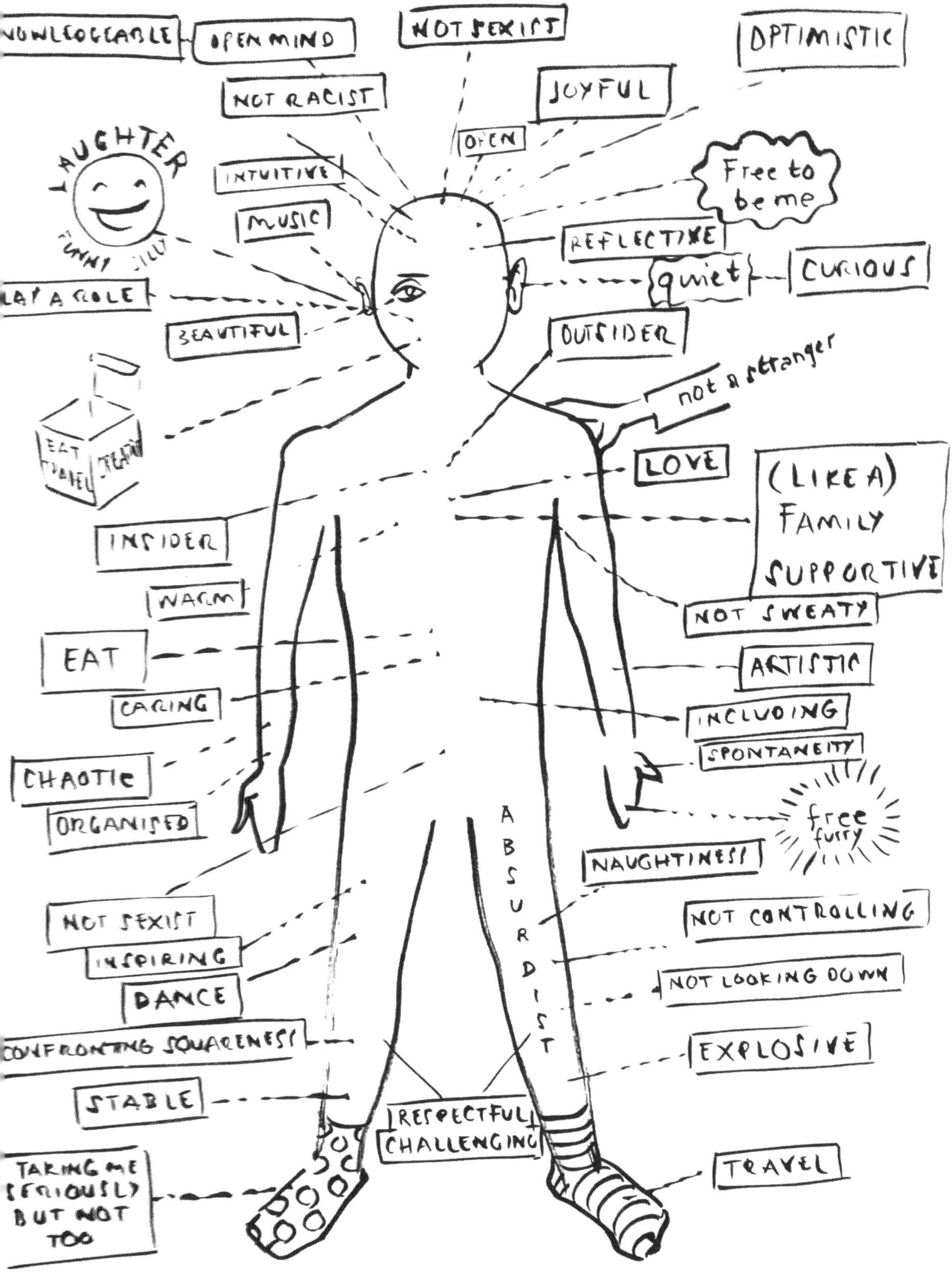
KNOWLEDGEABLE
OPEN MIND
NOT SEXIST
OPTIMISTIC
NOT RACIST
JOYFUL
LAUGHTER
FUNNY SILLY
OPEN
INTUITIVE
Free to be me
MUSIC
REFLECTIVE
PLAY A ROLE
quiet
CURIOUS
BEAUTIFUL
OUTSIDER
not a stranger
EAT
TRAVEL
DREAM
LOVE
(LIKE A) FAMILY SUPPORTIVE
INSIDER
WARM
NOT SWEATY
EAT
ARTISTIC
CARING
INCLUDING
SPONTANEITY
CHAOTIC
ORGANISED
free furry
ABSURDIST
NAUGHTINESS
NOT SEXIST
NOT CONTROLLING
INSPIRING
DANCE
NOT LOOKING DOWN
CONFRONTING SQUARENESS
EXPLOSIVE
STABLE
RESPECTFUL CHALLENGING
TAKING ME SERIOUSLY BUT NOT TOO
TRAVEL

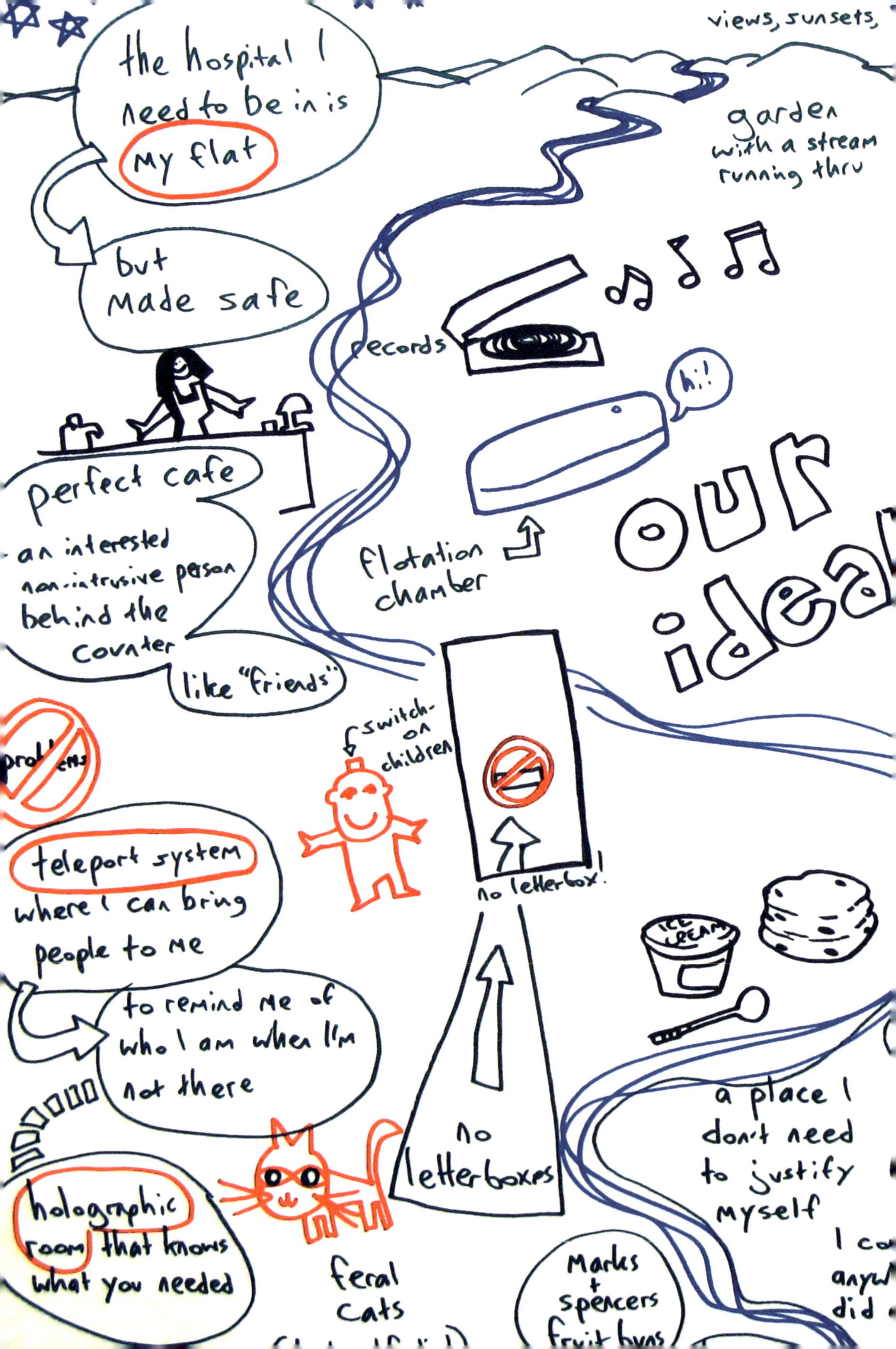
views, sunsets,
the hospital I need to be in is my flat
but made safe
garden with a stream running thru
records
hi!
flotation chamber
our
idea
perfect cafe
an interested non-intrusive person behind the counter
like "friends"
problems
switch-on children
no letterbox!
ICE CREAM
teleport system where I can bring people to me
to remind me of who I am when I'm not there
no letterboxes
a place I don't need to justify myself
holographic room that knows what you needed
feral cats
Marks + Spencers fruit buns

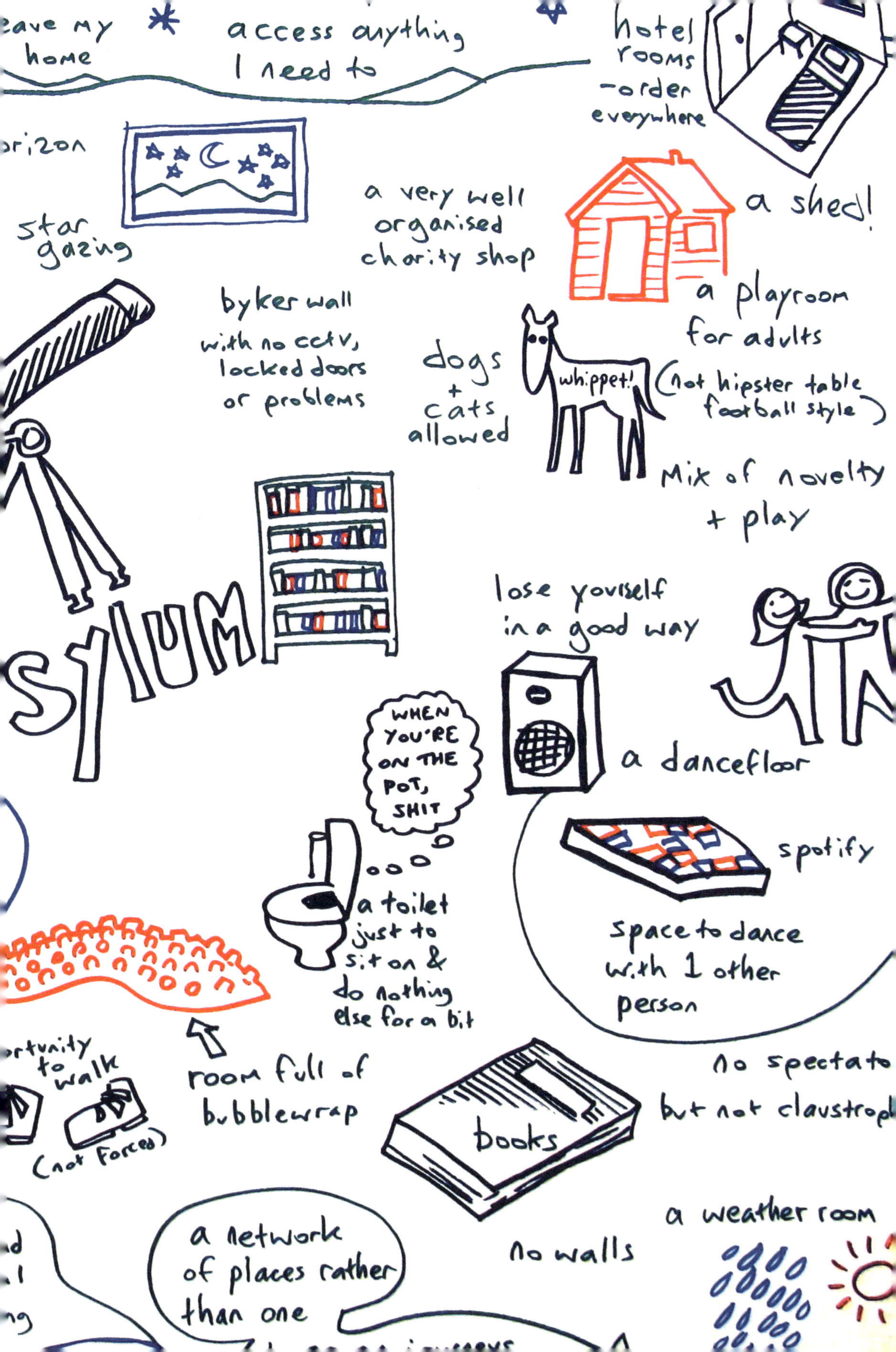

access anything I need to
hotel rooms - order everywhere
star gazing
a very well organised charity shop
a shed!
byker wall
with no cctv, locked doors or problems
dogs + cats allowed
whippet!
a playroom for adults (not hipster table football style)
Mix of novelty + play
SYLUM
lose yourself in a good way
WHEN YOU'RE ON THE POT, SHIT
a dancefloor
spotify
space to dance with 1 other person
a toilet just to sit on & do nothing else for a bit
room full of bubblewrap
to walk
(not forced)
books
a weather room
no walls
a network of places rather than one

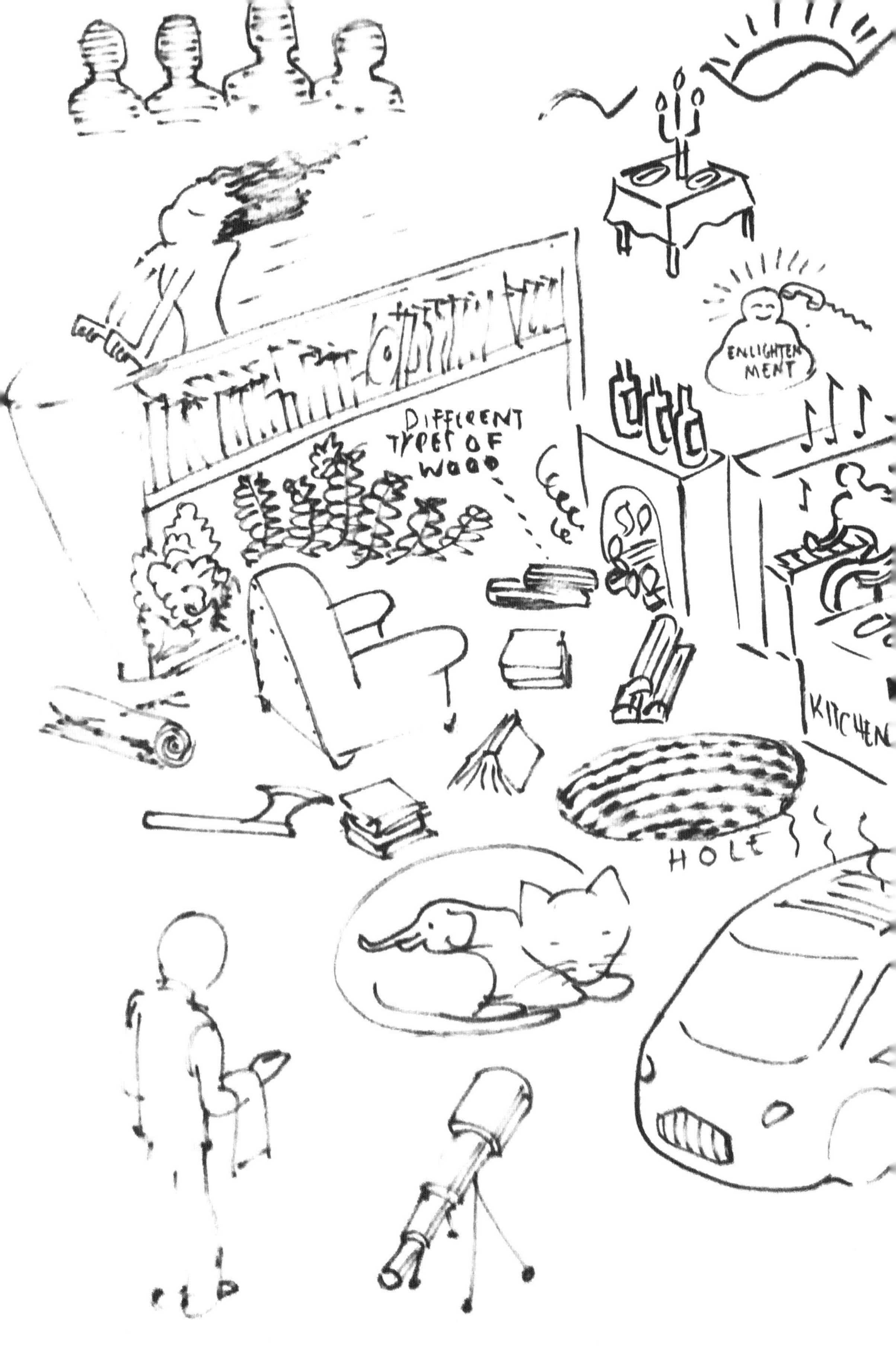

ENLIGHTEN MENT
DIFFERENT TYPES OF WOOD
KITCHEN
HOLE

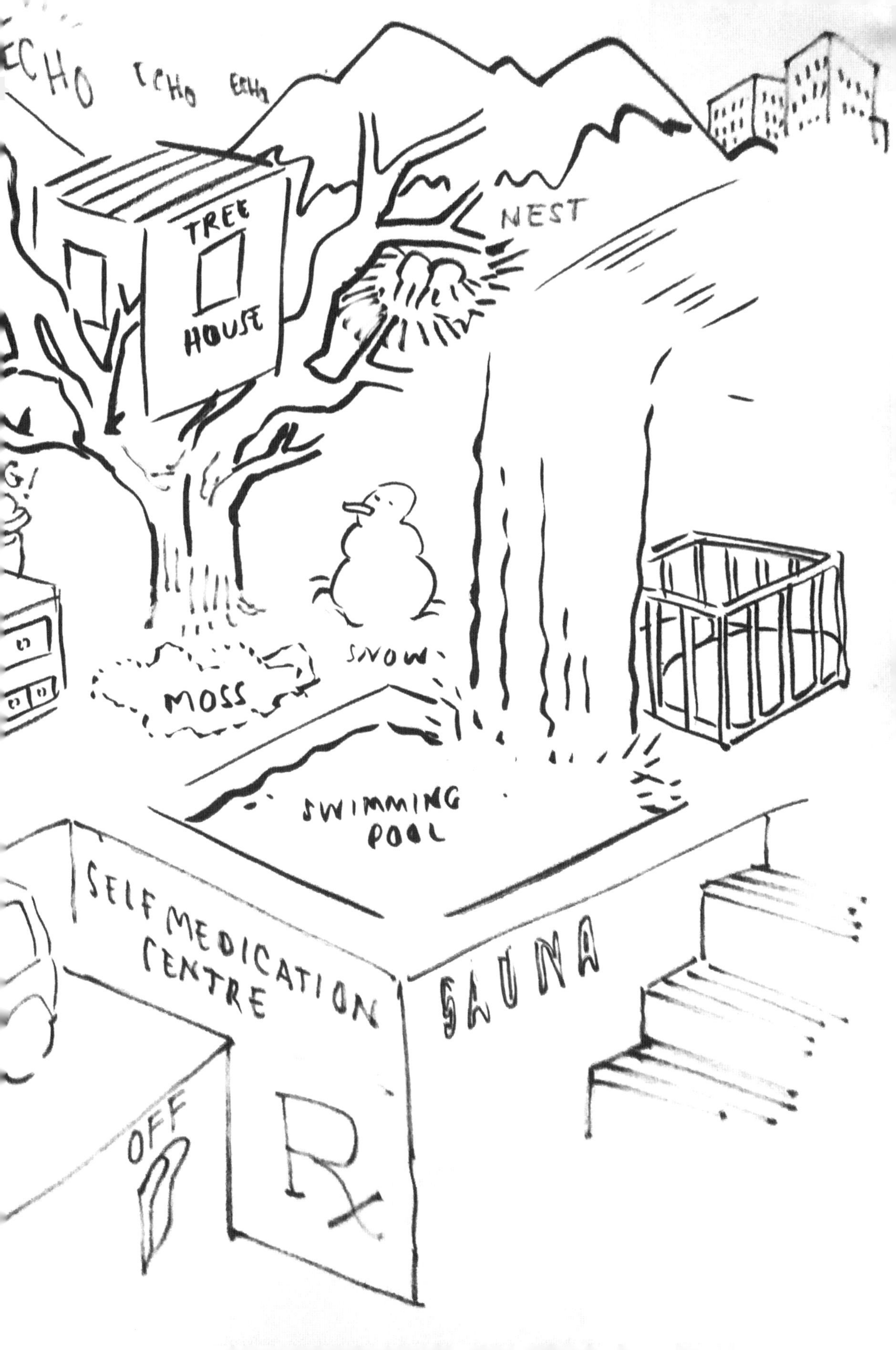
ECHO
ECHO
ECHO
TREE HOUSE
NEST
SNOW
MOSS
SWIMMING POOL
SELF MEDICATION CENTRE
SAUNA
OFF
G!

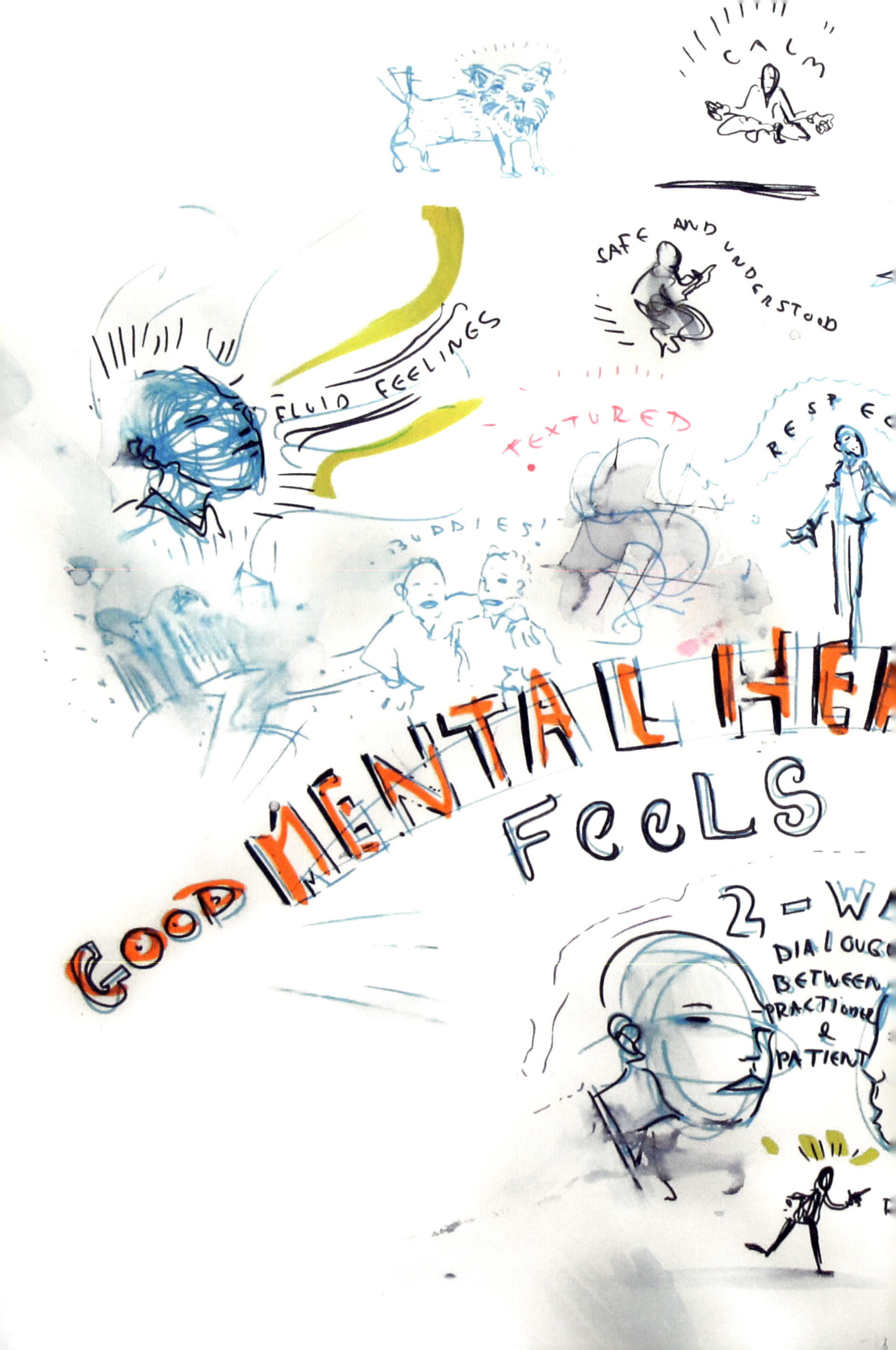
CALM
SAFE AND UNDERSTOOD
FLUID FEELINGS
TEXTURED
RESPEC
BUDDIES!
GOOD MENTAL HEA
FEELS
2-WA
DIALOUG
BETWEEN
PRACTIONE
&
PATIENT

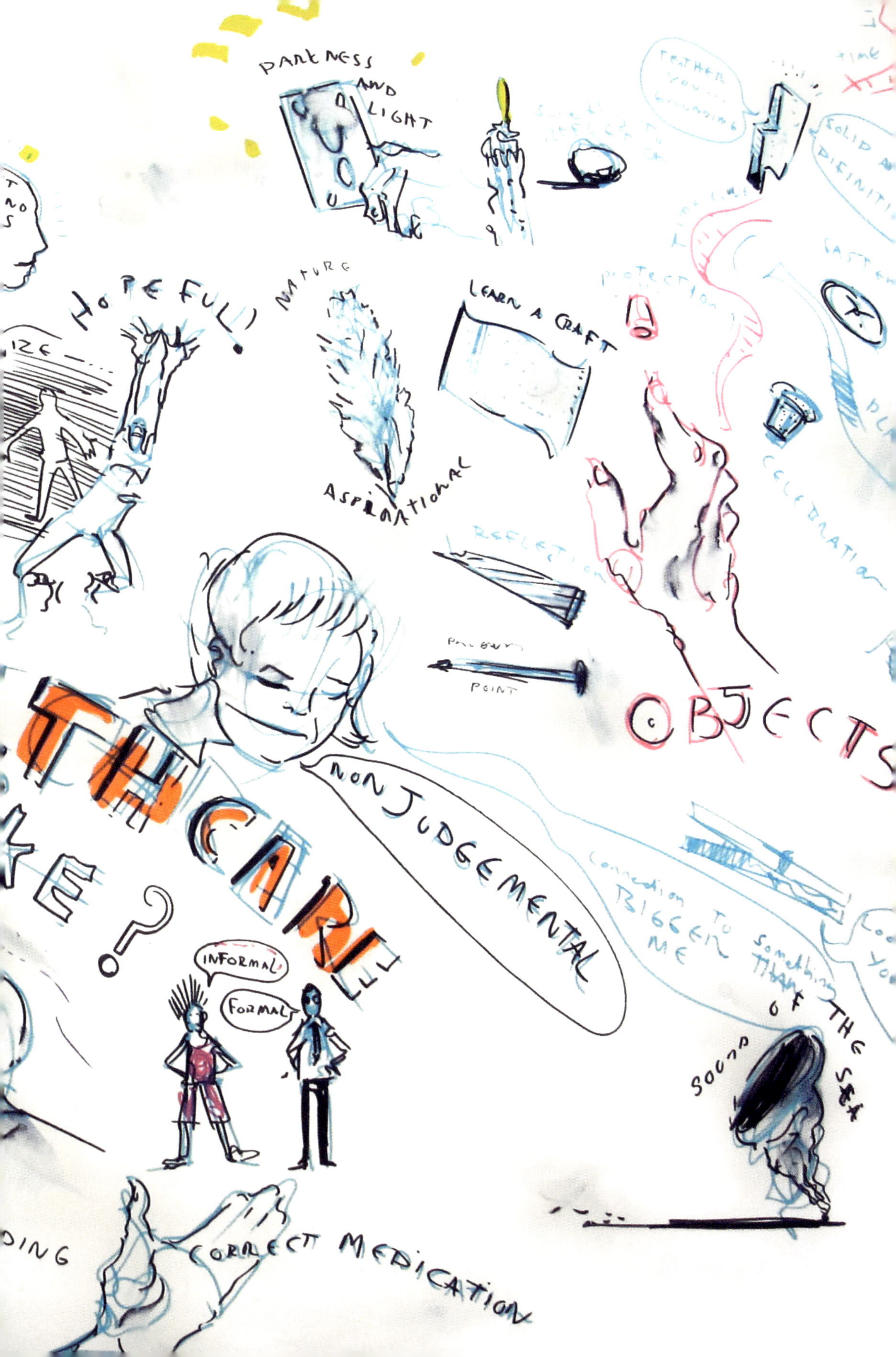
DARKNESS AND LIGHT
HOPEFUL!
NATURE
ASPIRATIONAL
LEARN A CRAFT
PROTECTION
REFLECTION
CELEBRATION
POINT
OBJECTS
NONJUDGEMENTAL
INFORMAL
FORMAL
Connection to something bigger than me
SOUND OF THE SEA
CORRECT MEDICATION

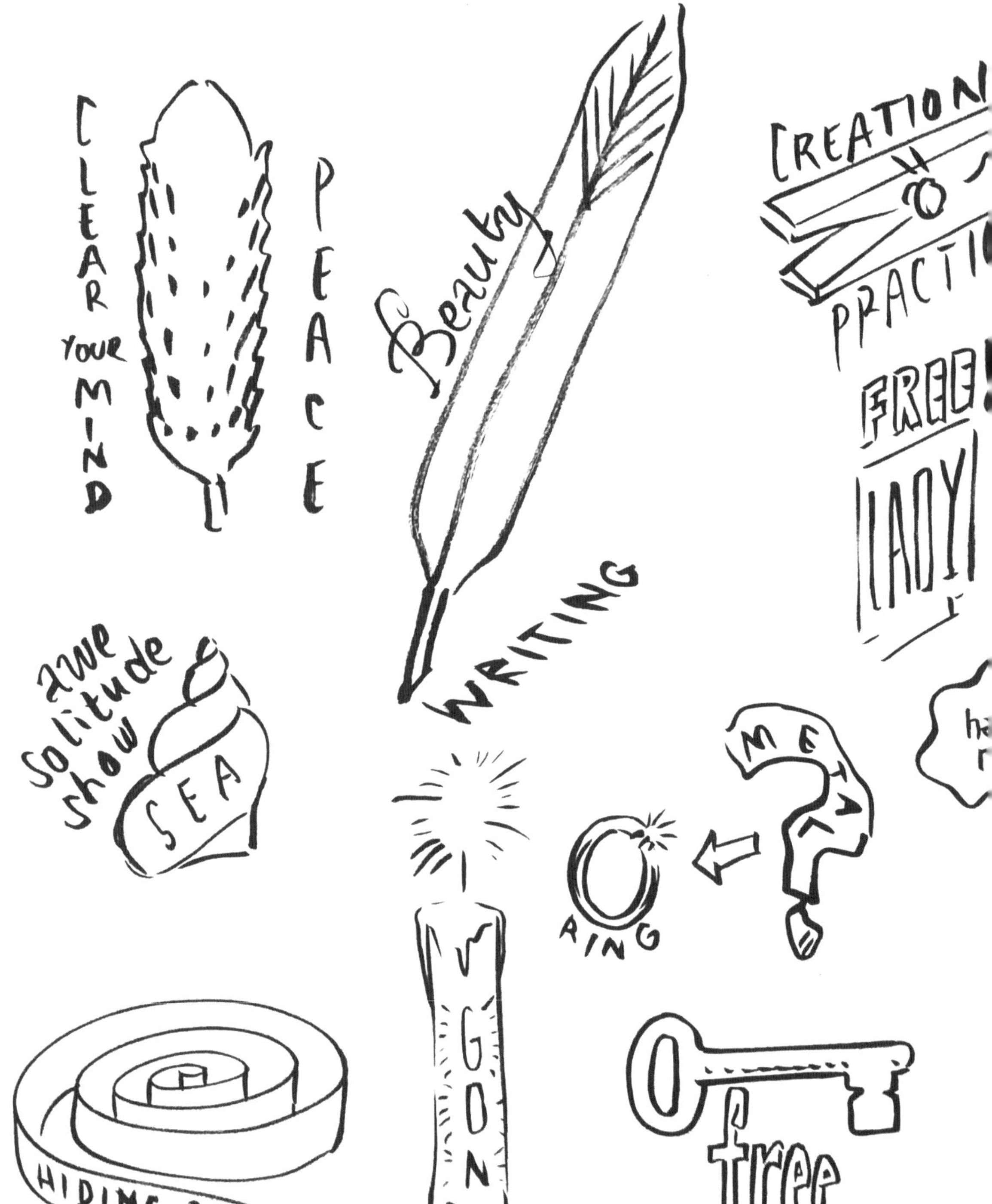
CLEAR YOUR MIND
PEACE
Beauty
WRITING
CREATION
awe
Solitude
show
SEA
METAL
RING
GONE
HIDING PLACE
free

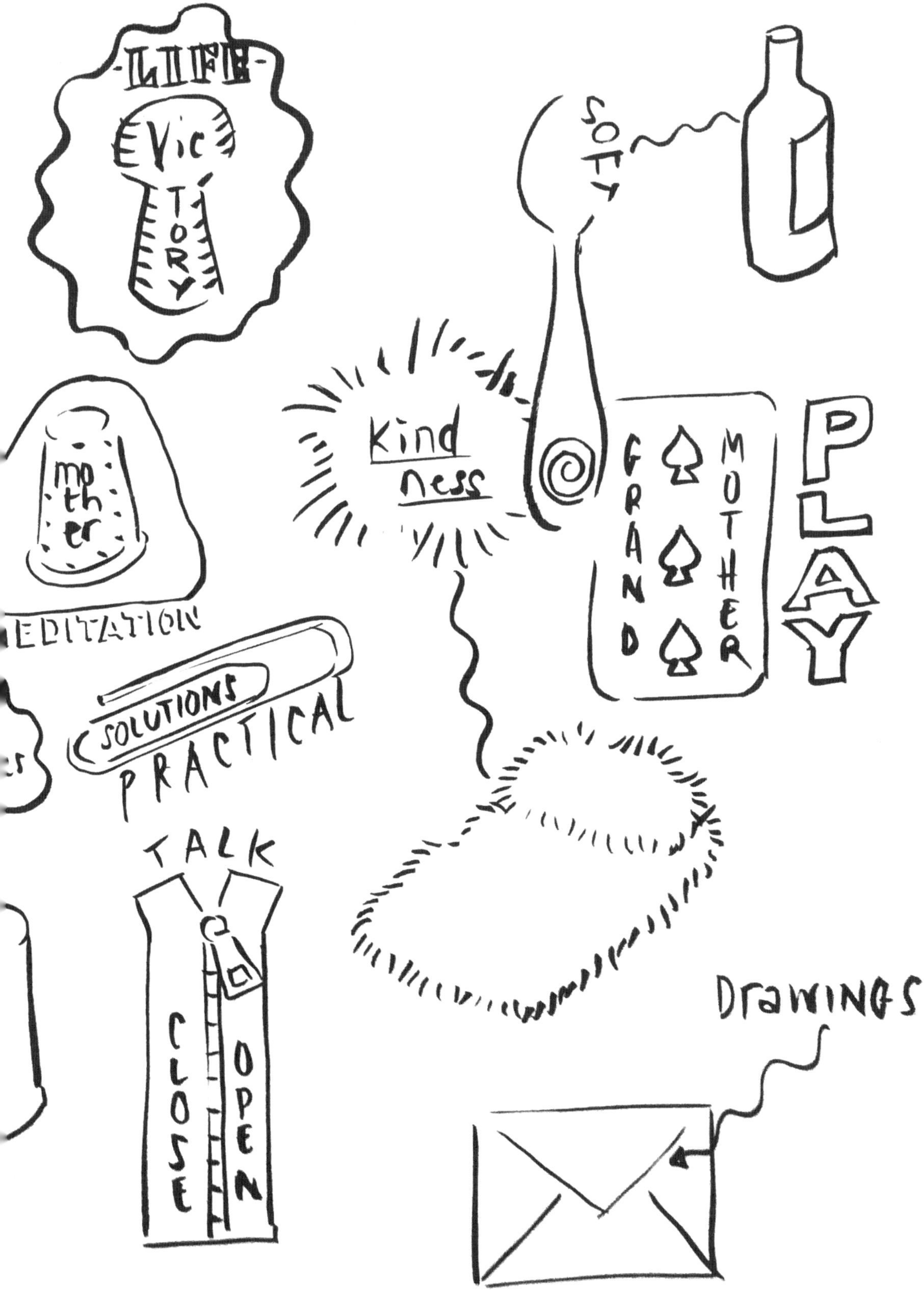
LIFE
Vic
TORY
mother
kindness
GRAND
MOTHER
PLAY
SOLUTIONS
PRACTICAL
TALK
CLOSE
OPEN
Drawings

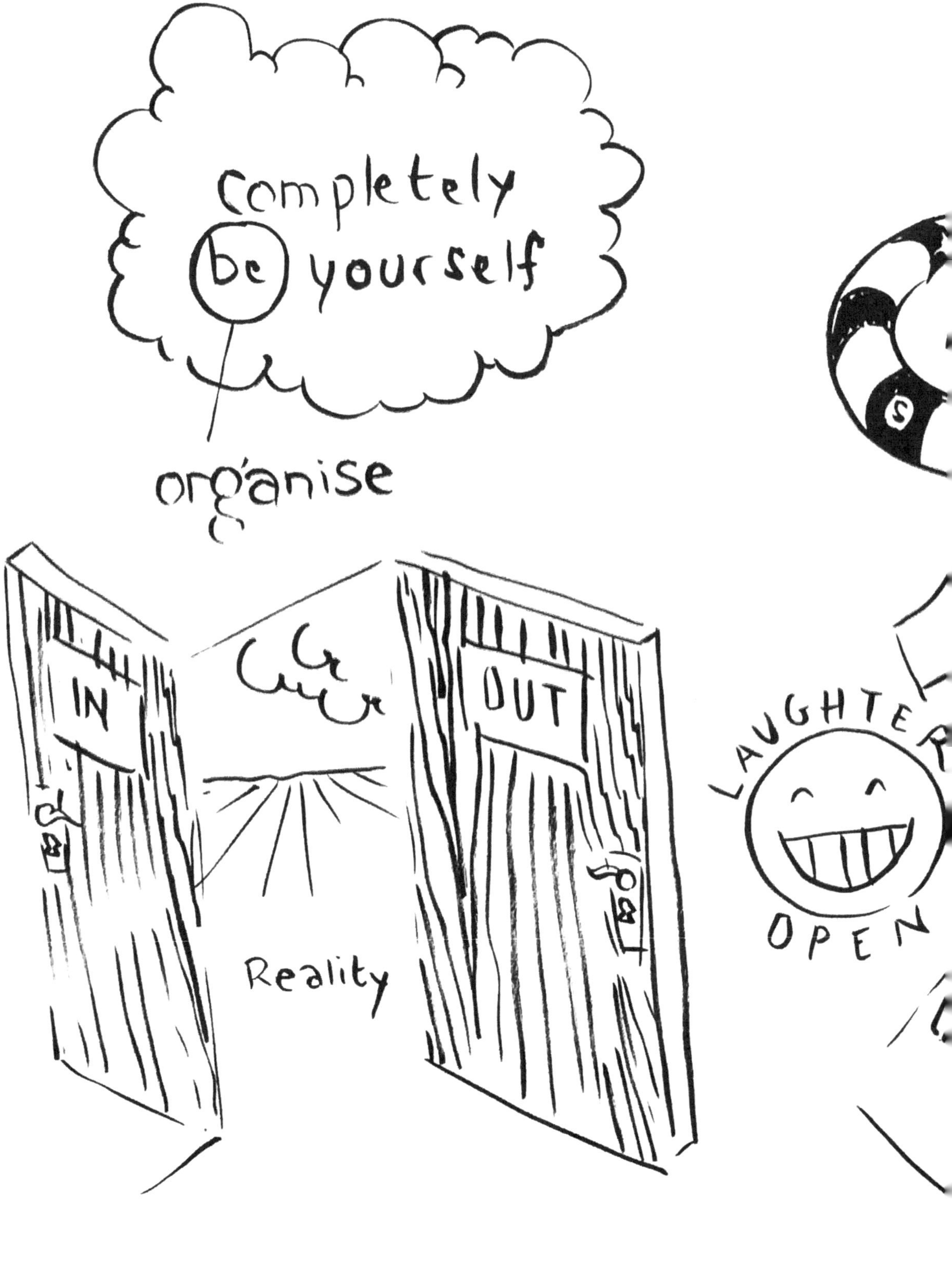
completely
be yourself
organise
IN
OUT
Reality
LAUGHTER
OPEN

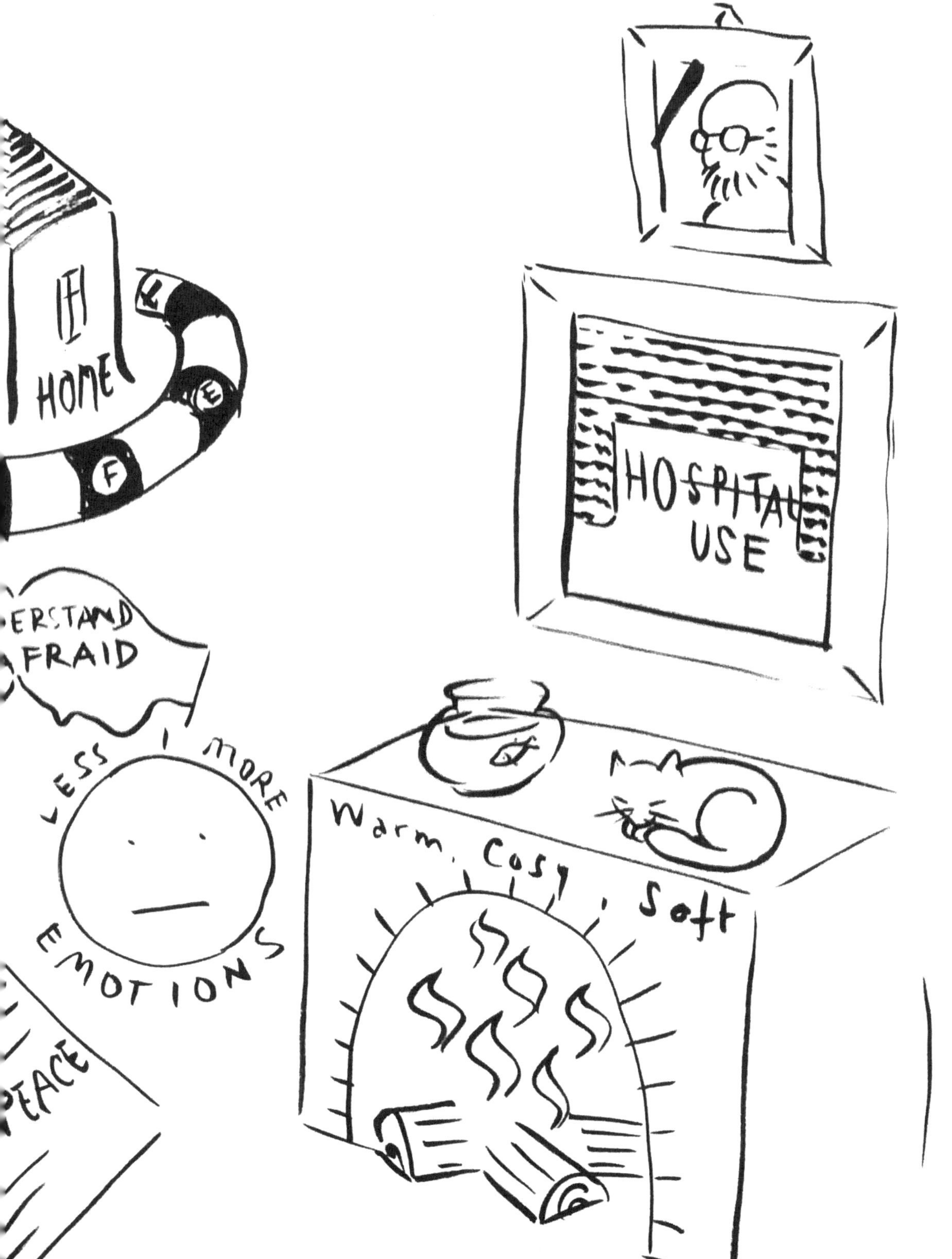
HOME
F
E
L
ERSTAND
FRAID
LESS
MORE
EMOTIONS
PEACE
HOSPITAL
USE
Warm, Cosy, Soft

56

CARING RELATIONS

We find the crystallisation of a dialogue between arts and health in the direct relationship between an artist and a patient. In many if not most art and health projects, the process of creating an artwork within a care-setting is as important as the product. Often, the performative process of creating relations is the artwork in itself. Nicolas Bourriaud defined this type of art, where human interactions and social values are central, as 'relational aesthetics'. In this practice, the artwork in itself exists in the ephemeral transient space that is created between the artist and everybody else present. Whether this momentum is generated through co-creation, interactive performances or artistic interventions that interfere with daily life doesn't really matter. It's the interaction, the way the artist touches audience and, importantly, the way the audience affects the artist, that makes this kind of work so valuable. We feel that this approach can be especially valuable in a care-setting, where the prolonged collaboration between artist and patient can lead to a deep understanding and relationship between both.

This is also a central theme in the work of the German choreographer/performance artist Vera Tussing. In her various performances and installations, she tries to create unique, interpersonal encounters between audience and performer, often through a multisensory experience. In the research 'Tactile Quartet(s)', string musicians replace their instruments with the audience members' limbs, giving the audience an added tactile dimension in their experience of the music. This research was split between two main strands, one focused on musical embodiment; the other on touch and tactile pathways. For this second strand she used choreographic trajectories formed by embroidered ribbons and costumes, which initiated choreographic engagement with the audience. These ribbons invite for a more spatial tactile experience and also reflect the collaborative research with the diverse group of guests at the TOPAZ day care center.

When I was first invited to contribute to IN/FINITY, I was in the midst of engaging in a field of research which I sometimes refer to as the 'Tactile Cycle' of my work. Through a series of thematically resonant, performative research experiments over a number of years, I explored the possibilities of dancers and musicians coming into direct, tactile encounters with the audience, and using those encounters to generate their movement and performance.

I organised my engagement with IN/FINTY and TOPAZ along a series of 'research threads', exploring different aspects of this 'Tactile Cycle'. The first of these, 'Tactile Quartet(s)', developed in collaboration with violinist Clara Levy and several of her colleagues from the Royal Conservatory of Brussels (Koninklijk Conservatorium Brussel), was an exploration of how music, sound, the production of embodied sound-making and the movements of the musician can be experienced via the medium of touch. The second thread grew from the duet 'Both, Two' that I created with the dancer Esse Vanderbruggen, exploring the possibilities of 'tactility from a distance' and performatic empathy.

However, it is the final two of these 'research threads', 'Tactile Scores' and 'Tactile Choreographies' which we will explore more deeply below.

Tactile Scores

'Tactile Scores' began as an engagement between tactility and musical scores. I embroidered the score for the piece 'Music for Pieces of Wood by Steve Reich' on strips of fabric. The 'audience'/guests could then trace the progress of the music with their fingers as they listened to the recording, creating a tactile experience of sound on the skin.

I have occasionally used embroidery as an element in my practice and am drawn to the efforts of artists like Louise Bourgeois, Tracey Emin and Ulla-Stina Wikander to re-envision and resituate needlework as an artistic practice—set against a long history of stereotypes and assumptions surrounding decorative art, feminine labour and 'domestic duties'. I am particularly attracted to Bourgeois' proposition that 'the act of sewing is a process of emotional repair'.

Interestingly, the set-up at TOPAZ allowed us to subvert exactly some of those stereotypes and assumptions. One archetypal scene in countless books and films is men retiring to smoke and discuss world affairs, while the women withdraw separately to perform the 'lesser' decorative tasks of stitching and embroidery. During my work in TOPAZ, it was exactly when some of the guests were smoking on the terrace that I was able to engage them in a creative process centred around my stitching. The tiny temporary communities that were formed by people on a cigarette break allowed a twin form of release and engagement to develop—smoking and stitching.

Tactile Choreographies

The idea of embroidery as a mode of generating choreographic trajectories was further developed in 'Tactile Choreographies' in collaboration with Esse Vanderbruggen and Jivan van der Ende. We embroidered instigating phrases on long strips of fabric: ‘Please do touch’, ‘Touchez svp’, ‘aanraken aub’, ‘7adi min fadlack’. These translations, provided by the guests at TOPAZ, reflect the different languages spoken at the centre.

We laid these strips of fabric out in specific patterns across the space, which audience members could then trace with their hands. This act of tactile ‘reading’ sets the audience in motion.

We then ‘embodied’ this concept, sewing these phrases into the actual costumes that Esse and I wore as performers. An audience member could begin with their hand on my shoulder and—as we moved while maintaining an interlocked position—they could trace the phrases from my body to Esse’s. Through this, the performers’ body and the audience’s receptive touch became the starting points of a tactile trajectory.

Stitching Tactile Relations

Touch situates us in space. It builds a sense of embodied connectivity within one’s kinesphere. You can experience touch directly, or you can achieve an empathetic relationality by observing touch occurring at a distance. Both ‘Tactile Scores’ and ‘Tactile Choreographies’ are an attempt to bridge these twin forms of tactile encounter.

When you work with touch in performance, it creates an evanescent dynamic whereby the piece only truly appears in the moment of performance, in direct relation to the audience. You can practice in an empty rehearsal room all you want, but without actual live, unpredictable audience members to react and generate movement, you will only ever be guessing what might actually happen when the piece is performed. This creates a situation in which the creative process is more a procedure of setting strategies, and the actual realisation of the work occurs in the precise moment of interaction. As Maria Puig de la Bellacasa writes in ‘Matters of Care’, touch is an ‘invitation to rethink relationality in its corporal character... engaging with touch also has political significance.... fostering haptic abilities as a sensorial strategy for perceiving the less noticeable politics’.

With this in mind, it was very important to me that I engage with the unique set-up of TOPAZ, rather than just placing my already-existing work in a new environment. Engaging in a completely new process at TOPAZ allowed us to shift between sharing different stages of our creative processes with the guests. Their input fundamentally informed how the work we brought with us was able to grow.

Research: Tactile Choreographies
Photos: Vera Tussing

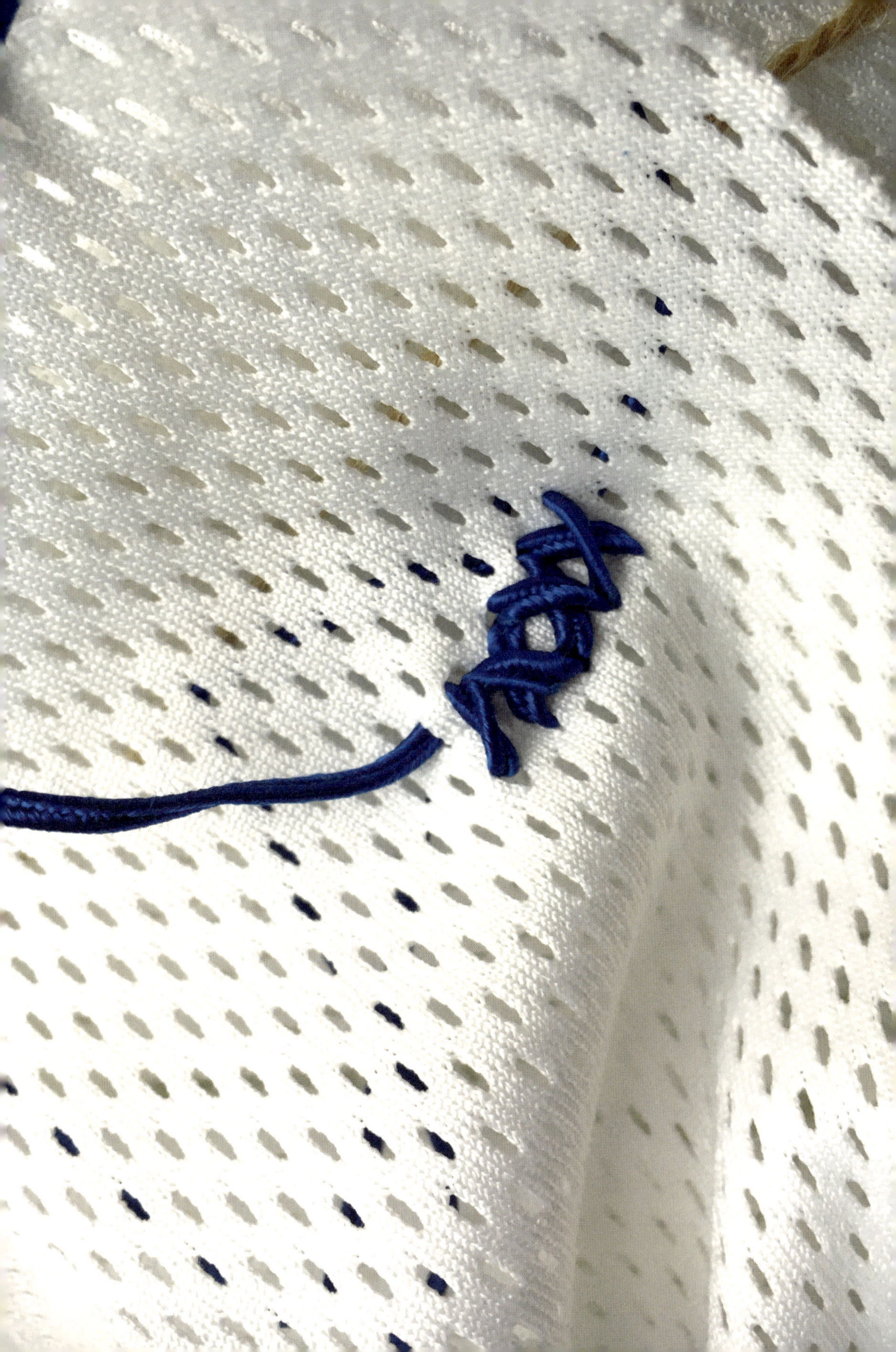

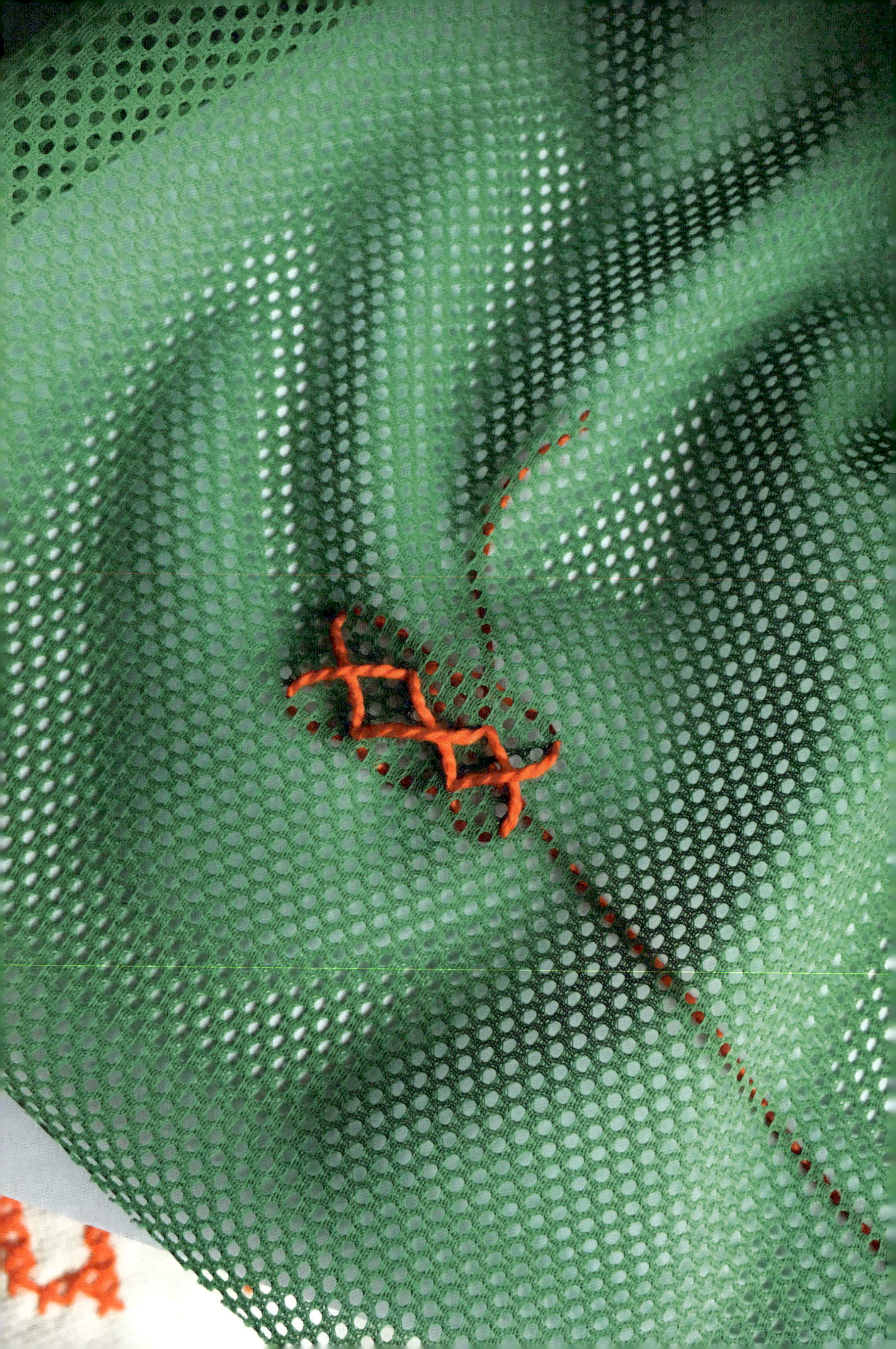

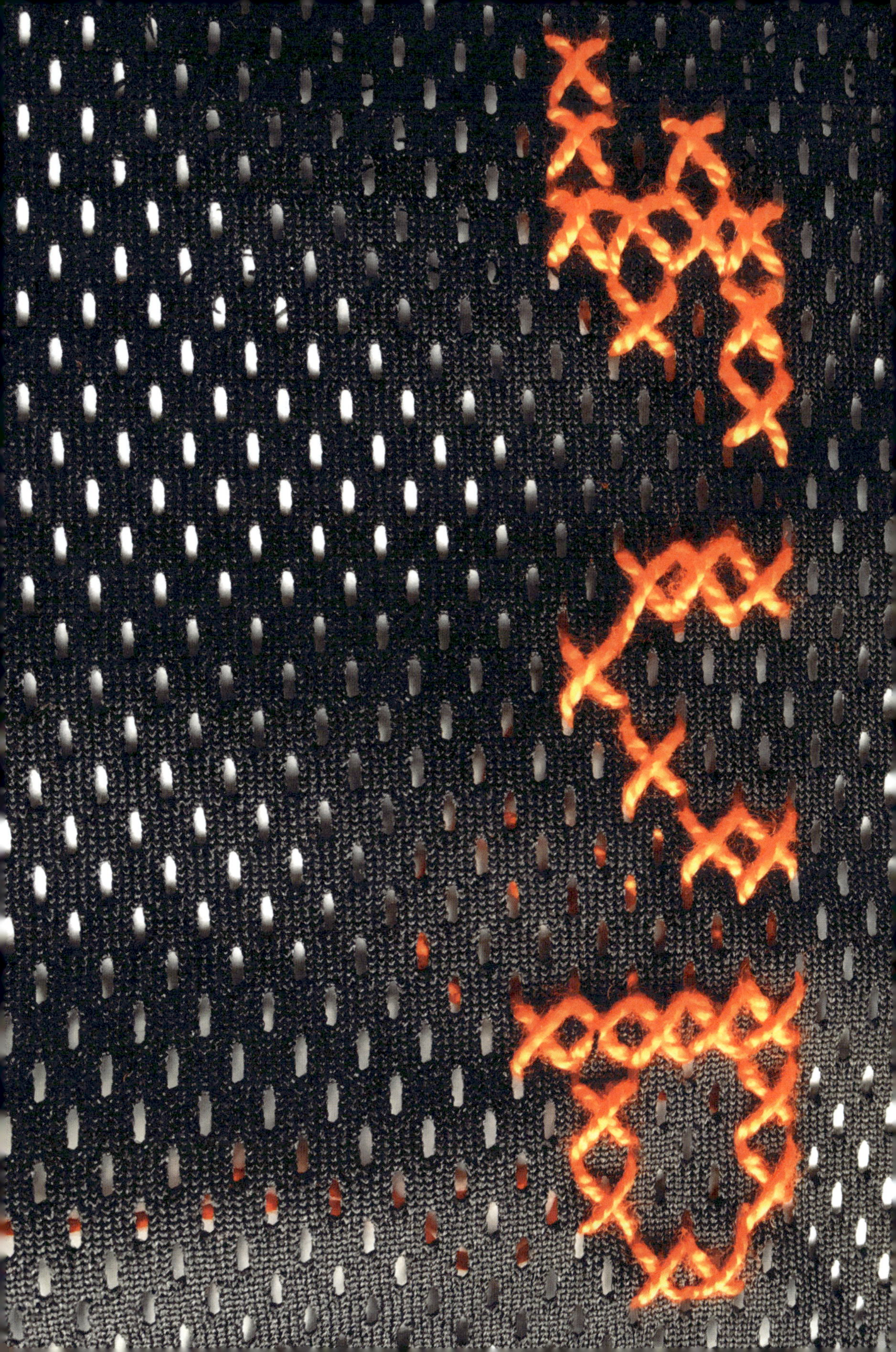

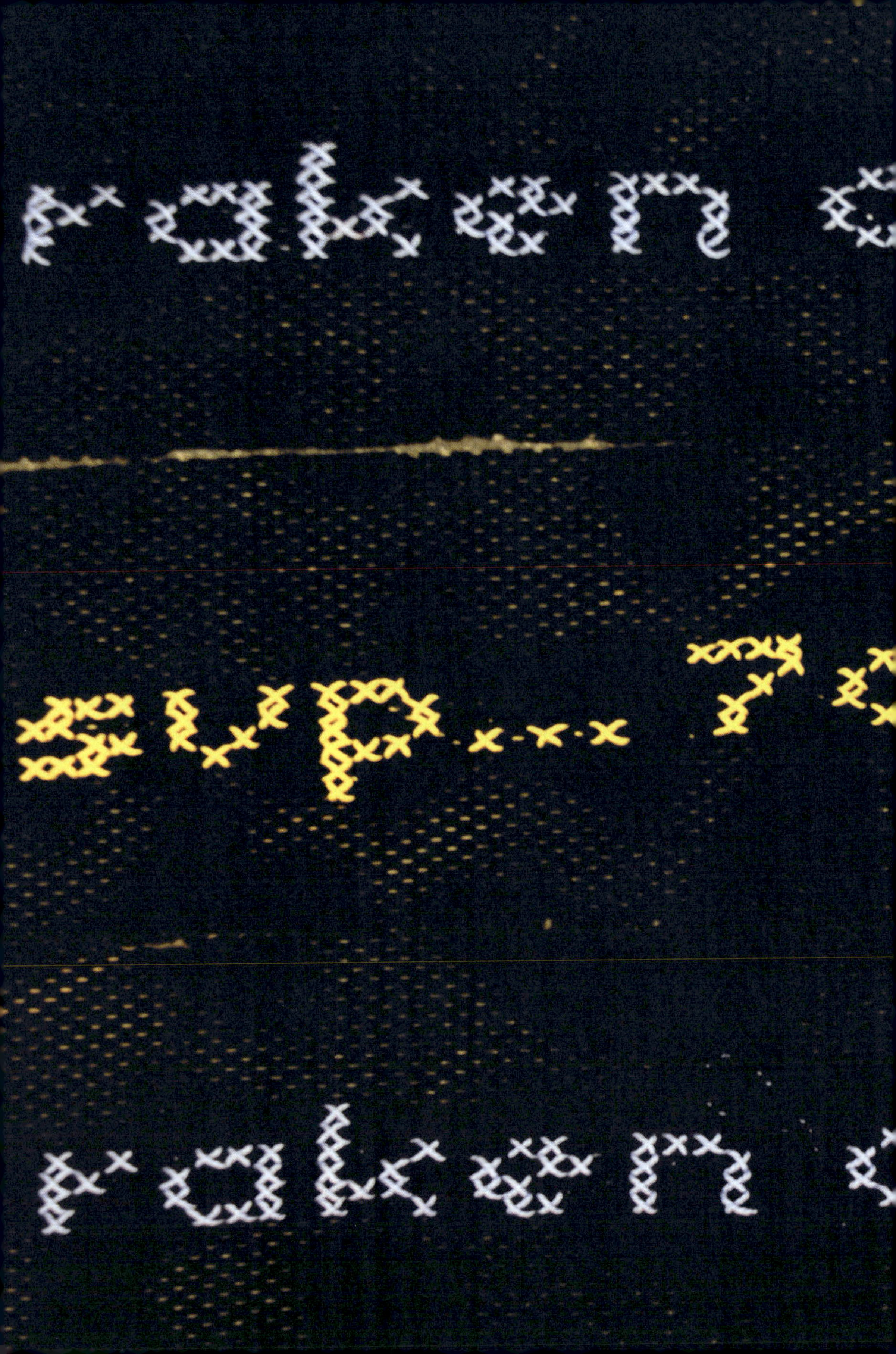
raken
sup
raken

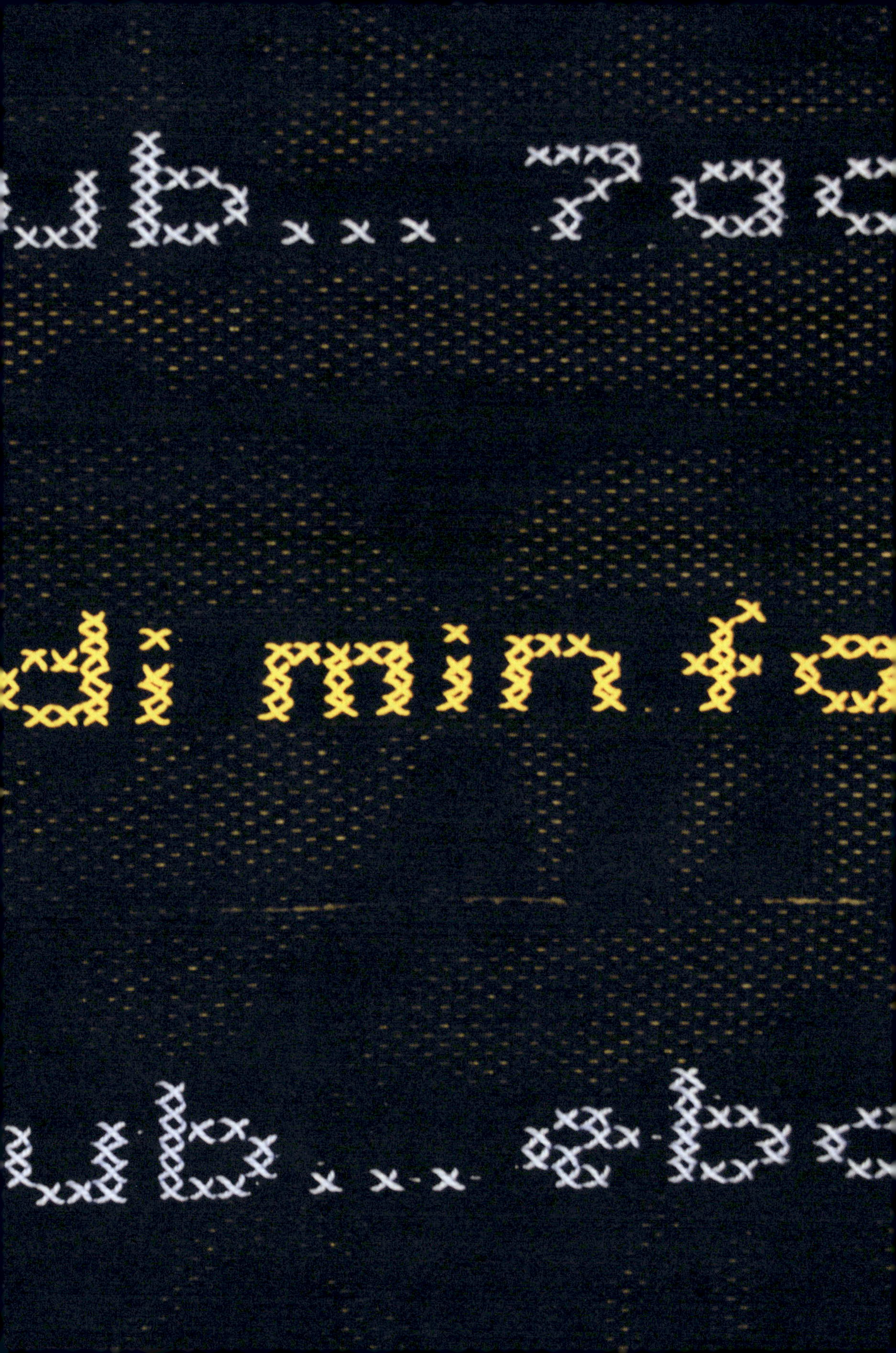
di min fo

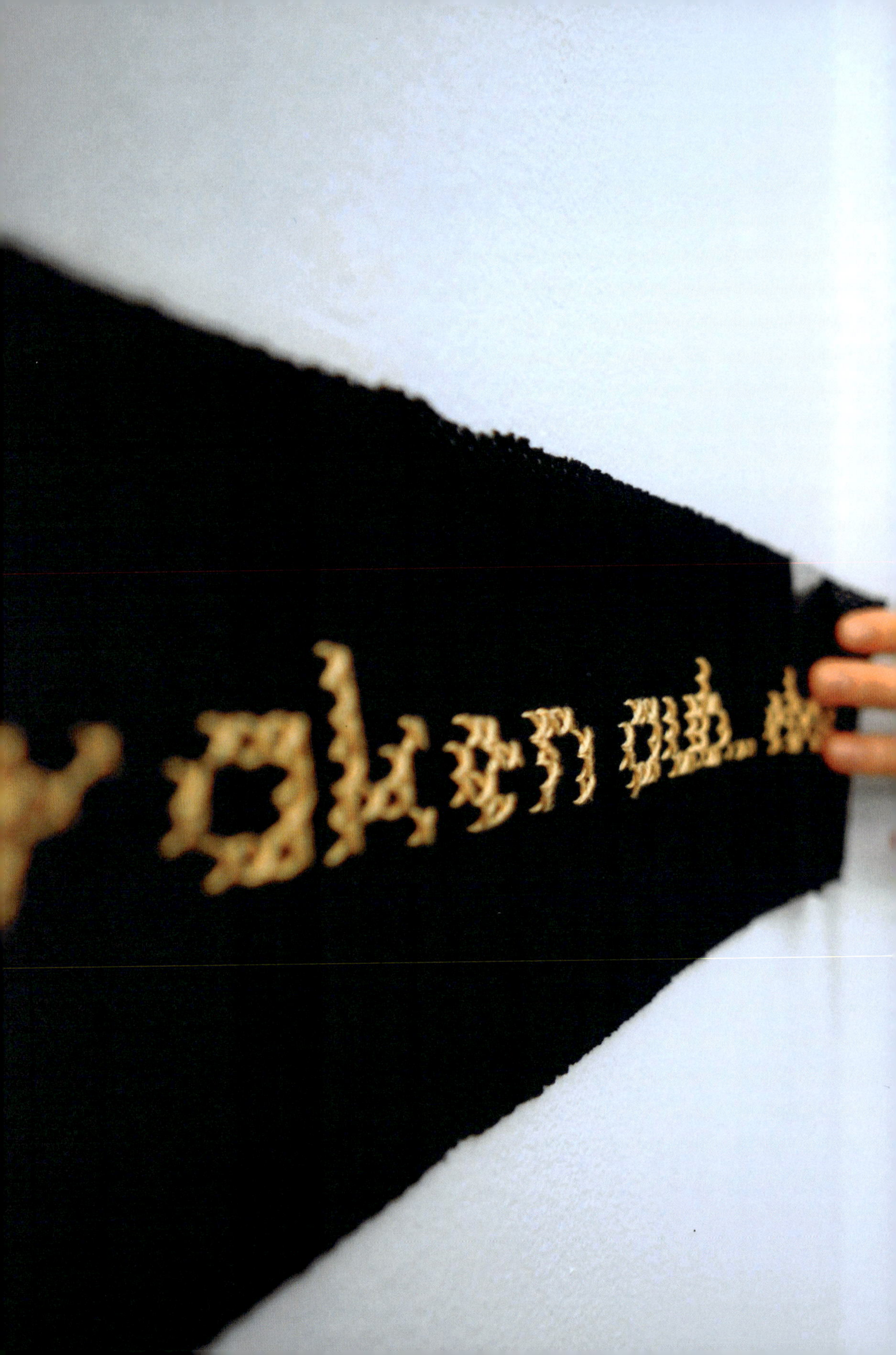

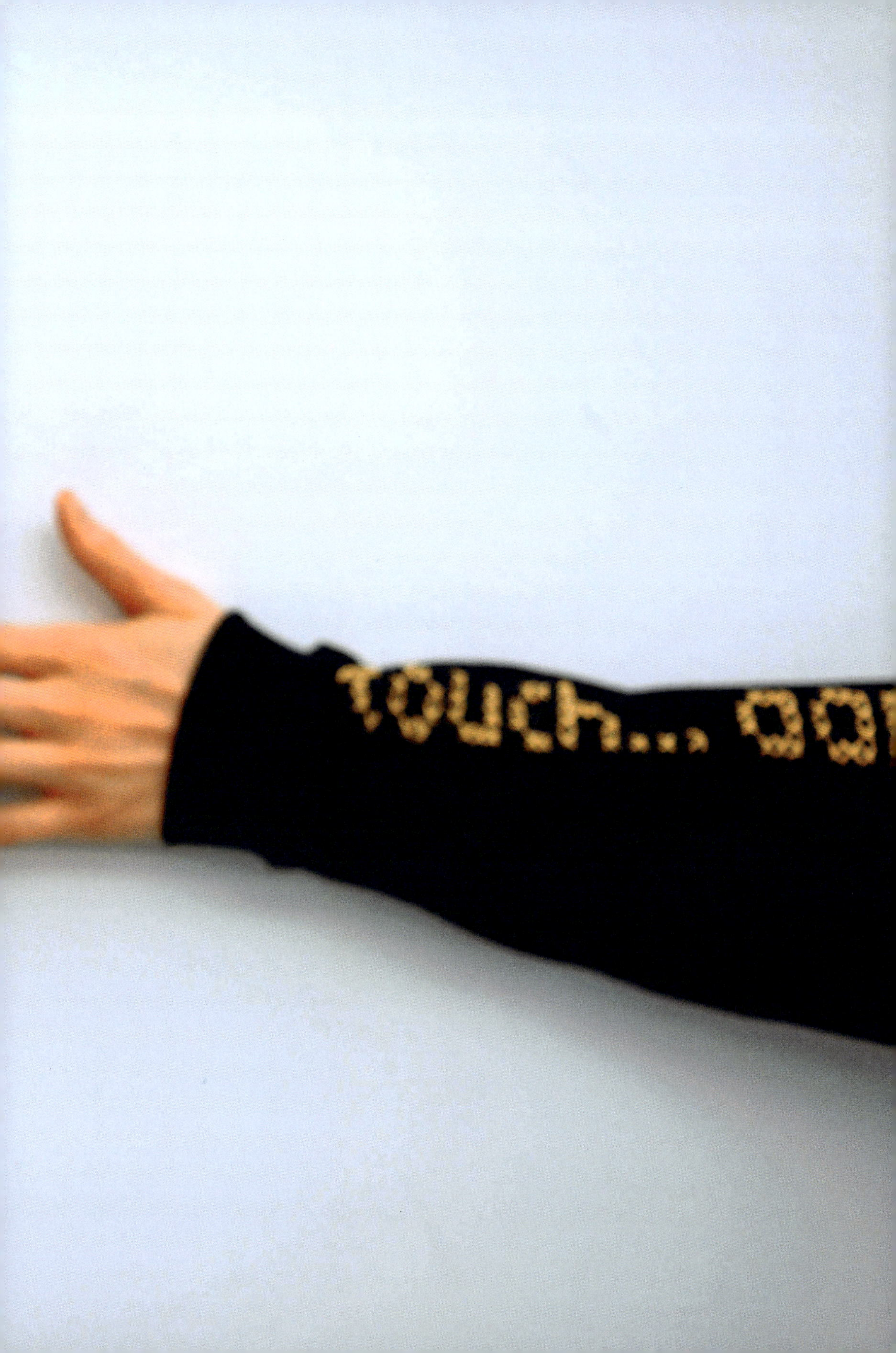
touch...

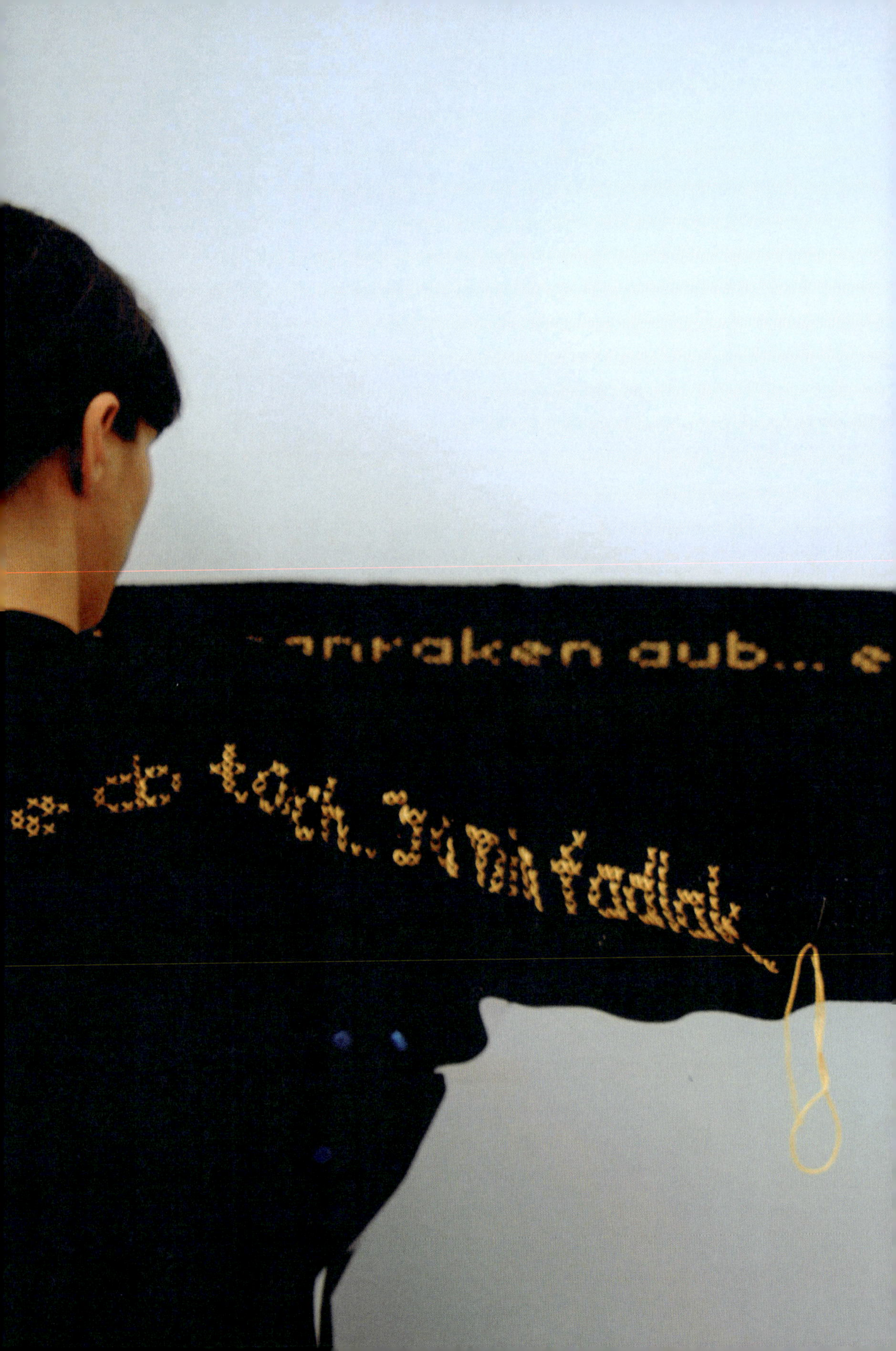

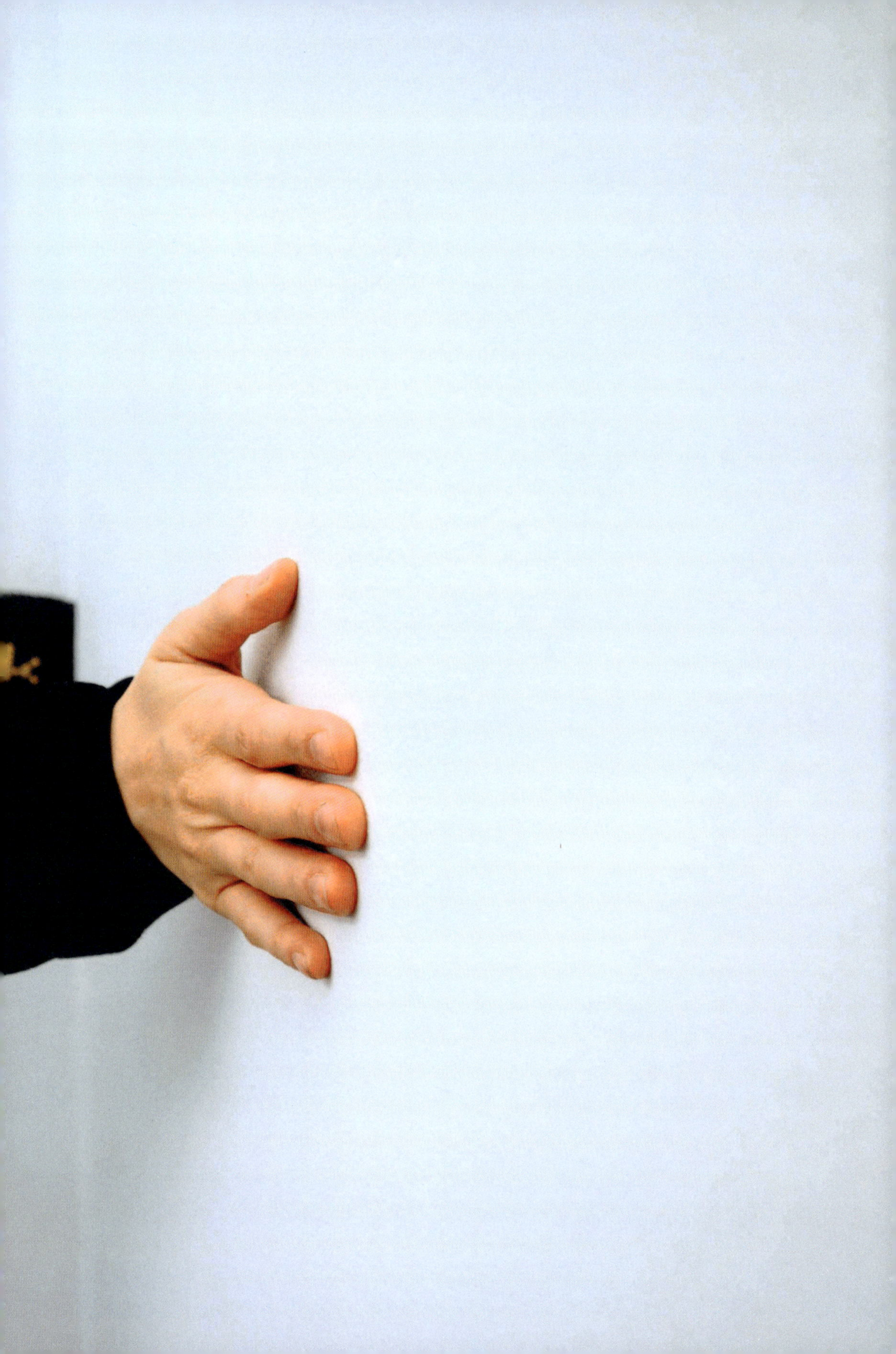

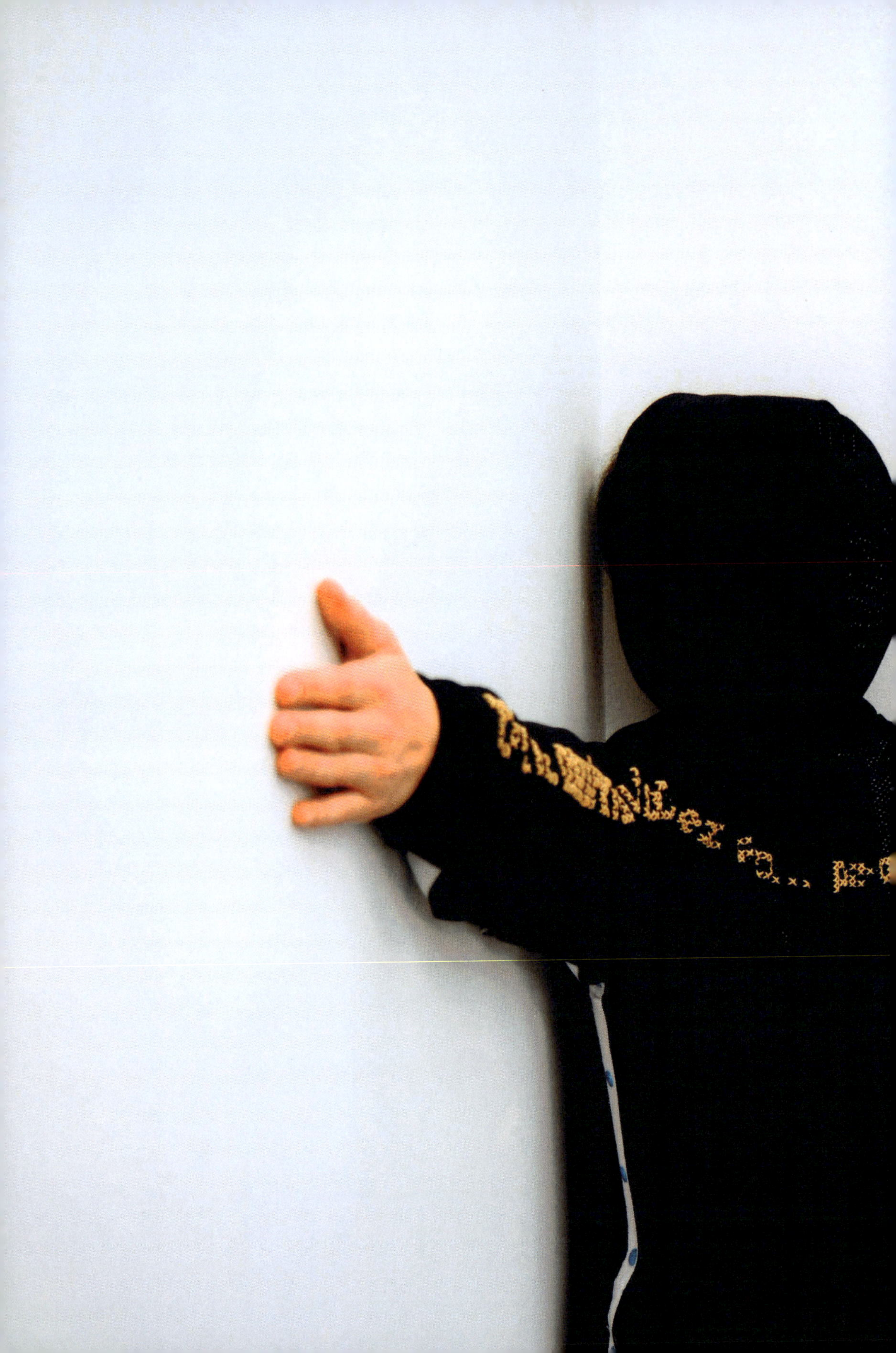

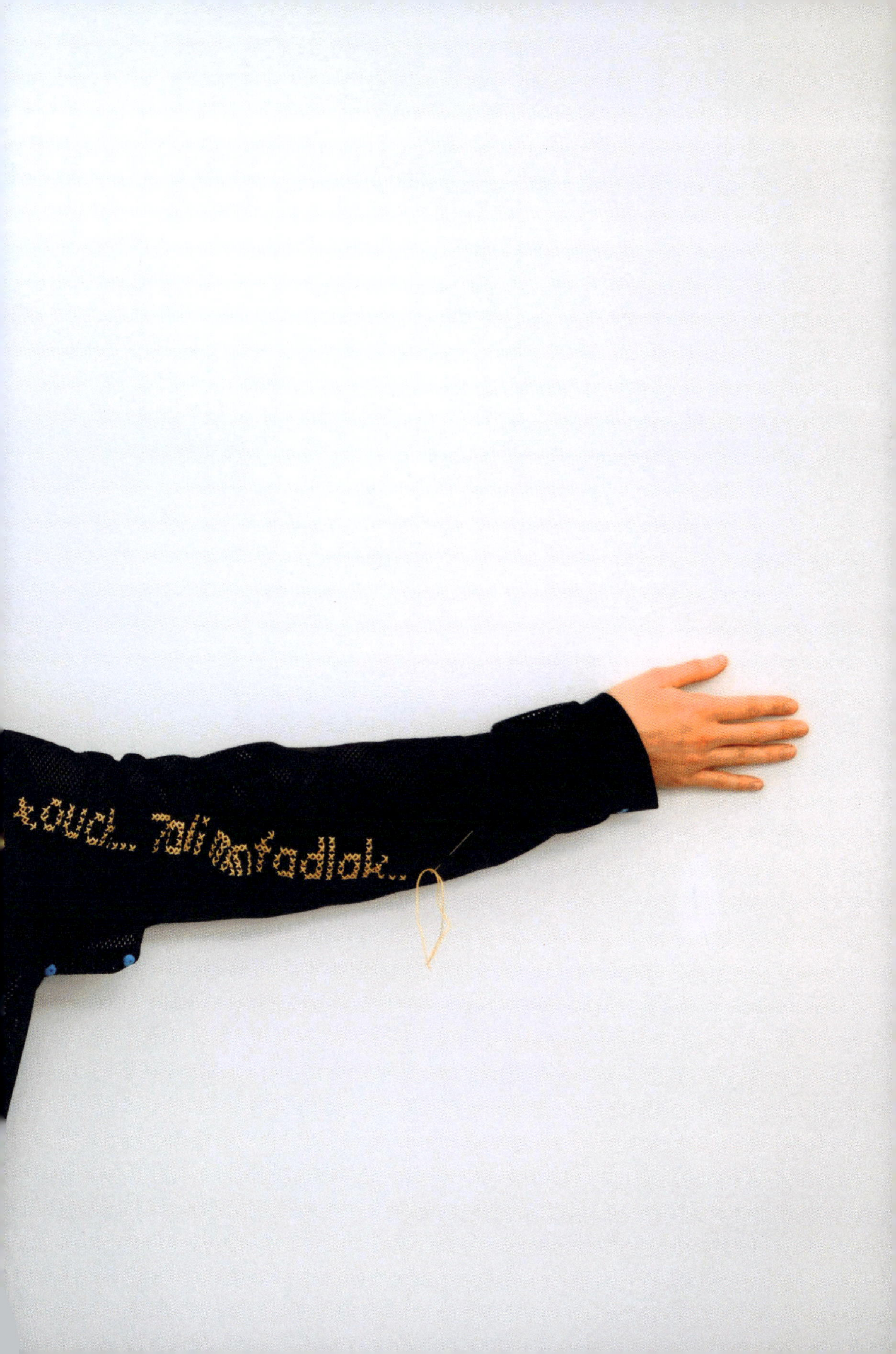

72

TRANSFORMATIONS

73

Does art change us? How does art change us? The interest the medical field shows in art often springs from a belief that artists can contribute to healthcare and health promotion. Medical researchers go to extreme lengths trying to prove that art has a beneficial impact on our health and well-being. Questions of which art might be beneficial (and which art might not be) and how art achieves these effects, remain largely unexplored. Are these the questions we should be asking, then? Such an endeavour can appear extremely reductionist, as it seems to only allow 'don't worry, be happy, hospital art'. It does not take into account the unique nature of art, nor does it do justice to its complexities. If art itself eludes all attempts at definition, how could it then be possible to identify the supposedly 'working ingredients' that art should possess? Perhaps a better approach is to start by questioning our pre-occupation with 'health' and 'transformation'. Recently the German theatre scholar Erika Fischer-Lichte explored the concept of 'transformation' related to art in her book 'Transformative Aesthetics'. We invited her for a conversation.

Transformations, a Conversation with Professor Dr. Erika Fischer-Lichte

Julie Rodeyns & Wouter Bouchez

‘In Germany, people are obsessed by the idea that theatre matters, that’s why it’s so much fun to research it: because the emotions behind it are so strong’, says Professor Dr. Erika Fischer-Lichte, who, through her fierce dedication and sincere enthusiasm proves to be an exemplary exponent of the German Theatre Tradition she has just described. We meet the director of the international research centre ‘Interweaving performance cultures’ (Freie Universität Berlin) to discuss the centre’s recent publication ‘Transformative Aesthetics’ (2017). It assembles essays on the transformative effect of art: an idea that, as the publication illustrates, is very old and familiar to cultures across the globe. Professor Fischer-Lichte is strongly convinced that theatre has a transformative power but thinks that ‘art on prescription’ is not a good idea. A conversation.

JR & WB:
The belief that art holds healing powers has grown quite popular recently. In his publication ‘Art is therapy’ (2013), philosopher Alain de Botton explores the question of what a museum visit is for. The title of his book leaves absolutely no doubt about his opinion on the matter. An abundance of scientific studies claim to provide evidence that art is beneficial for people’s health and well-being. Such studies have already inspired regional and national governments worldwide to take action. To give just one example, in several Anglo-Saxon countries, so-called ‘art on prescription’ programmes, in which doctors not only prescribe drugs but also museum visits, are on the rise. We were grateful to learn about the concept of ‘transformative aesthetics’, as—to our understanding—it provides a tool to historicise this current interest in the beneficial impact of the arts on health and well-being. What was your motivation in developing this theoretical concept?

EFL:
To me, the aspect of transformation seemed key with regard to theatre. At the same time, it is overlooked in most theories of aesthetics. Nietzsche, who talks about it a lot, is perhaps the exception. I thought that we really ought to talk about this transformative potential that art can have. I found it fascinating to assemble essays on different theories from the past as well as from different parts of the globe: the idea that art has transformative powers is hardly a Western concept!

JR & WB:
Can you explain in what way this concept is key to Western theatre?

EFL:
There is a very long tradition of believing that theatre does something to you; that it makes you a better person. Different theories share this idea of transformation, but they focus on different kinds of transformation. First, there was Aristotle, who took the concept of ‘catharsis’ from medicine. I can also refer to Schiller and his idea of ‘Bildung’, meaning that a human being should develop his or her

potential to the fullest. Art helps you to do this. Before Schiller, in the 18th century, the plays of Lessing and the introduction of realistic psychological acting at that time can count as an example. We have numerous accounts that, during Lessing's first domestic tragedy, the audience sat silent for three and a half hours—very uncommon at that time—and all were in tears! For Lessing, a tragedy's aim was to arouse empathy. In his opinion, the best human being is an empathic human being and art helps you to achieve this.

JR & WB:
In contrast, was theatre sometimes also considered to be bad for people's health and well-being?

EFL:
Absolutely. At times, people believed that the devil was behind theatre. In the 17th century, the Puritans in England prohibited theatre because they thought that theatre was causing harm by raising emotions that shouldn't be raised. In that regard, theatre is different from, for instance, literature. There's good or bad poetry, but poetry was never considered to be good or bad in itself. Theatre, however, has always been surrounded by people who thought it was either great or horrible. Of course, we need to understand this in the context of different traditions. In the States, theatre is perhaps mostly regarded as entertainment, while in Germany, people are obsessed by the idea that theatre matters: that it can have enormous impact and make you a better person.

JR & WB:
Is it also your personal conviction: can art change us for the better?

EFL:
I very strongly believe—and this is also what I have experienced with audiences in all these years that I have been going to see theatre—that the confrontation with art, any kind of art, changes something in a person. However, unlike Lessing or Schiller, I would never dare to say in what direction, or to what effect. I'm extremely careful in that regard.

JR & WB:
How do you understand it, then?

EFL:
If we look at today's art, most art has a 'liminal quality'. For the time that you are listening to music, looking at a painting or sitting in the theatre, you are in a state beyond the ordinary and enjoy things that you perhaps wouldn't enjoy when they happen in real life, or the other way around. This is already a very important quality in itself: that you are taken away from your normal life. It is also the prerequisite for art to have an impact but—and this is very important—that impact is not predictable. It does not work as Aristotle had imagined: that theatre arouses pity and fear in all spectators and that they will all experience the same transformative catharsis. How people cope with art's liminal quality is very individual. Even for two persons from the same country, the same culture, the same class, who grew up in more or less comparable ways, it will not work in the same way. Also, these are not

transformations that endure; usually they don't. After experiencing the liminal space in which art places you, you can go back to your former self again. Perhaps there is something that you will carry with you, but this won't be the same for everybody and it won't have any lasting effects. We therefore have to use the word 'transformative' in a very careful way.

JR & WB:
What about Applied Theatre, a practice that usually engages so-called 'vulnerable' individuals or communities as active theatre makers? Often, it explicitly states as its primary goal the empowerment or transformation of its participants by tackling issues related to public health, education, social welfare, equal rights, criminal justice....

EFL:
In Applied Theatre, everybody involved is aware that there's a certain goal. As an artist, you can rule out certain kinds of aesthetics that you know won't work and try out aesthetics that you hope will work for the goal in mind. You can deduce from the wording I use that it's rather problematic. Perhaps, in certain traditions or very particular kinds of theatre, art can be used for a very specific purpose, for instance, to obtain more self-confidence. For instance, in the case of Kenyan writer and theater maker Ngũgĩ wa Thiong'o, when he started using the local language Kikuyu instead of English, he suddenly had access to the peasants. It did something to them, for sure, but what was this something? If you grow up in a country where as a child you're being blamed and mocked at school if you don't speak English well, perhaps it does something to your self-esteem when a performance is brought in your own language and you feel that you are being taken seriously as spectator. However, this is very particular to this unique case!

JR & WB:
Applied theatre is often understood to be at odds with the concept of art for art's sake: an idea that was introduced in the 19th century and still prevails in contemporary art, which expresses the belief that art is autonomous and should not serve any political, moral, didactic, utilitarian or other end. There seems to be an inherent tension between the concept of autonomy on the one hand and that of transformation—as implying an instrumentalisation of the arts—on the other hand. How do you understand these two notions together?

EFL:
First of all, in Germany, we don't make the distinction between theatre and applied theatre, which is typical for Anglo-Saxon countries. Instead, we use 'theatre' as a very broad umbrella term, including many different kinds of theatre, with different profiles, and all working differently. In my opinion, all have the potential to transform people, but in different ways. However, theatre should always be political: not in the sense of addressing political issues, but in the sense of being critical, making people aware of things. For instance,

from its founding in the 1960s, youth theatre in Berlin was simultaneously very funny and very critical in addressing patterns of sexual behaviour: laughing about the 'normal state' made clear that it was actually a 'ridiculous state'. In other words: theatre can have different goals—in this example, an educational goal—but always within the framework of autonomy: the idea that you can do (almost) everything under the umbrella of art is holy in this country. In that regard, the notions of autonomy and transformation are not contradictory to me, on the contrary. It's exactly the concept of art for art's sake that allows for a liminal situation: you can, so to speak, sink back into your innermost being and immerse yourself in the artwork, exactly because it should not have any purpose, or relate to your social situation.

JR & WB:
Your interpretation of the concept of 'transformation' seems to differ from the many medical studies that seek to generate evidence that art is beneficial to our health and well-being, which implies an instrumental understanding of art.

EFL:
Indeed. As I understand it, it does not have a particular goal. Art takes you out of your normal self - a break from your normal routine - and puts you in a state of in-between. When that happens, art has done what art can do. However, you can't predict or repeat what will come out of that. A performance that makes one person happy might leave somebody else angry. We have to let go of the idea that you can prove that it works and that, once proven, it will work on everybody. I would never dare to propose that.

JR & WB:
Can you understand why the medical world is preoccupied by the idea that art can have a beneficial impact on health and well-being and why it strives to prove this?

EFL:
Of course, I can understand the appeal. Searching for a cure is typical for the mind-set of a doctor. However, while with tested medications there's a reasonable probability that they will work, with art you're always on unstable ground. You can't look at art like it's a kind of particular medicine, this is not how art works, in fact, this is to abuse art. It doesn't say anything about art, it only tells us something about those who want to use art for purposes for which it is really not meant. I'm not denying that there may be individual cases in which one specific patient, confronted with a specific work of art, suddenly feels a strong impact. However, you will never be able to deduce general rules. One shouldn't raise expectations about what art can accomplish, which it can never fulfil.

JR & WB:
How should we interpret the studies claiming that art is beneficial for health and well-being, then?

EFL:
It shouldn't be surprising that, when an artist works with them, this helps

people who are in a vulnerable state and who perhaps don't get a lot of attention. I do think that most artists have this sensibility, to sense what is going on with this or that person. When an artist enters a health-care context, remains open, shows respect and interest, and makes people feel that they count as a human being, that's already quite something! However, it's not because it's art that it works, but because they are addressed as a person instead of a patient: this is what is healing, liberating, not art as such!

JR & WB:
Does that mean that, in your opinion, there is no place for art projects in healthcare?

EFL:
I am aware that using the arts for healing purposes is a very popular idea. I think that it's a very interesting but also a very complex topic. Who should be healed of what, by art? One first has to clarify that. It reminds me of a recent debate I attended at a university museum. They wanted to remove some artworks from a show because the idea came up that seeing these works might disturb the well-being of the students. Why this concern with well-being? Why can't students be confronted with disturbing facts? Life is full of disturbing facts. If we try to put everybody in a state of well-being, what good would that bring? On the other hand, while I believe that for 'normal' people it can be healthy to be provoked and see how to cope with it, how much you should provoke people that are already vulnerable remains another question.

JR & WB:
What approach would you propose?

EFL:
I think that you have to put in a lot of work, just to find out in each case, what would—hopefully—be the way to obtain a good result. You have to be open and willing to try things out. I can give an example: the performance 'Kunst und Gemüse: Theater ALS Krankheit' by German theatre director Christoph Schlingensief. On stage, in the middle of the auditorium, was a person, Angela Jansen, who was suffering from ALS. She could only communicate with others through eye movements, which were registered by a computer that translated it for us, the audience.

She told us about her fight with the health insurance company, which at first hadn't been willing to pay for the computer because she had less than four months to live. So, as spectator, you knew that this was going on a few weeks before her death. You could tell from her utterances that Angela Jansen felt very well in this situation where she could communicate to so many people about what troubled her and was taken seriously. She clearly enjoyed receiving all this attention. This may have had a certain effect on her, but again, while some people come to themselves when exposed to the gaze of others, others find it deeply troubling and would prefer to hide! Most of all, this performance had an effect on the spectators and perhaps, in a sense, was mainly a healing cure for them.

JR & WB:
How do you mean? In what sense?

EFL:
At first, among the spectators, there was a feeling of unease. Death is something which is shut out in our society today. For some people, it might have been a shocking experience to be suddenly confronted with a person who is very close to death. However, you could feel how the atmosphere gradually changed as the realisation grew that this is not shocking, but part of human life. Life comes to an end and here is a person who gives us the opportunity to experience with her what it means to be so close to death. It's hard to describe, but all of a sudden, there was a certain serenity amongst the spectators, as we supported her in this process of—well, yes—dying. I found this very beautiful, very meaningful, but how you achieve that, that's another question.

JR & WB:
How did Schlingensief achieve it?

EFL:
This was one particular moment in which Schlingensief succeeded in doing something that he, as an artist, was great at: looking at the otherwise 'invisible' people whom you don't normally see—the sick, the homeless, the migrants...—and making them visible. I think that this helped not only the actors, but the spectators as well. For me, performance is perhaps one of the most humane art forms because it works with 'us': our body, our soul, we are there, together, both actors and spectators. This is in contrast with the visual arts: when I stand in front of a painting, the work is not affected by what I imagine, feel or think. In performance, both parties are affected by each other.

JR & WB:
It seems to require a particular sensitivity, as a theatre maker such as, for instance, Schlingensief, to put vulnerable people in such a position. Where do ethics come in?

EFL:
Doctors would have advised against it, for sure. For me, there is something ethically challenging in this kind of work. In my opinion, you cannot do it just for art's sake; it must be both for the arts and for the patients' sake, which was obviously the case for Angela Jansen.

JR & WB:
An important rule in healthcare is 'first do no harm'. Is art in a medical context possible, if, following this principle, you have to be sure not to harm the patient or put a patient in a situation of risk?

EFL:
In that case, we might as well forget the whole thing!

JR & WB:
Because art always involves risk?

EFL:
Yes, but also because this is a lot of responsibility to give the artist and a tricky situation to put the artist in: the artist can never know what will come up. You don't know, and you can't know in advance. Humans are not robots....

81

82

83

84

85

86

87

THE DOCTOR

Despite their increasing popularity, art-care collaborations in healthcare contexts remain limited. Initiatives usually come from a doctor or healthcare professional with a special interest in art. Perhaps they once cherished the ambition to become an artist, or perhaps they still practice art on a non-professional level. Some, however, refer to a personal encounter with art that they experienced as particularly significant or even transformative. Based on this personal experience of art, they suspect that art can also be of value to others, such as their patients. For example, the chapter 'Space for Caring' in this book discusses the value that Prof. Dr. Erik Thys attaches to his artistic residency programme in psychiatry. In this chapter, we present the story of oncologist Prof. Dr. Wim Distelmans, one of the pioneers of end-of-life care in Belgium. He was, together with Sabien Bauwens, the initiator of the palliative and supportive day care center TOPAZ, where, from day one, art was embraced and given a special place. Here, the collaboration between art and care is based on the principle of mutual respect between the two fields. This offers a counterbalance to the cliché of doctors who consider artists as divas, full of good intentions but causing more harm than good. Even physicians who take a more moderate tone often consider art solely as a means to achieve positive health gains instead of acknowledging the specific nature of art. As a testimonial to a very personal relationship with art, the story of Distelmans underlines the importance of focusing on individual narratives, as the very diversity of the impact art has on different people may be what is most significant.

The Director
Wim Distelmans

THE AUDIENCE LEAVES THE MOVIE THEATRE AND THINKS: 'SOMETHING HAS CHANGED INSIDE OF ME. That film broadened my vision of the world.'

In another lifetime, I'm the director of a film like that: a film that strikes a chord, that speaks to a wide audience, that kindles the viewer's social engagement and indignation at abuses. Indignation is the engine that drives me. I have always wanted to be a filmmaker who is able to shatter people's fixed perspectives. For my fourteenth birthday, I asked my father for an 8mm camera.

I titled my first film 'De eenzaat' (The loner). It was a film born of indignation. Theo was a boy in my class. He was overweight, and was bullied and excluded. I couldn't understand why everyone was picking on him. At night, I dreamed up the scenario. In bed, in a daze, I wrote down the images in my mind in a notebook:

(1)

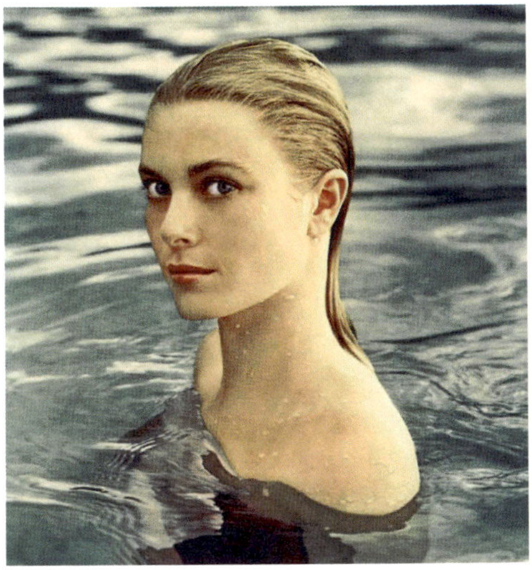

Theo being bullied by a stuck-up kid. He hears the schoolchildren shout after him: 'Fatty!' In the bicycle shed, Theo finds a scarf. The most beautiful girl in the class had lost it there.

(2)

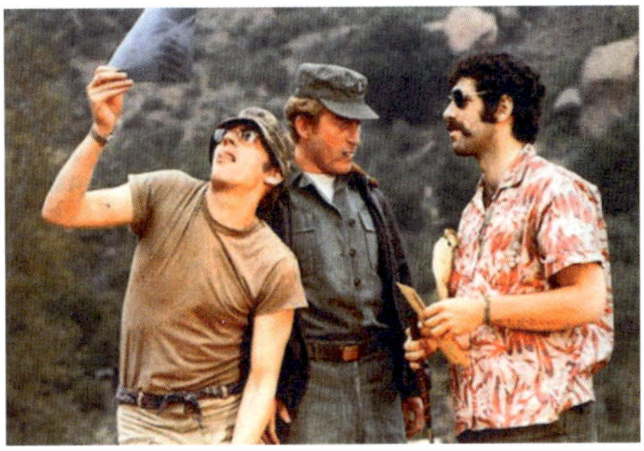

You see the girl frantically looking for her scarf. Theo brings it to her. She gives him the warmest look he can imagine—he's never had a warm look from anyone. The stuck-up kid falls from grace and Theo bikes back home down the willow-lined country road with a blissful smile on his face. I already had the ending in mind. I made that film with my classmates as the actors. After that, Theo wasn't bullied anymore. As for the most beautiful girl in my class, I was in love with her. It never worked out between us.

A year later I made a second film: 'Kalverliefde' (Puppy Love). I was shy and enjoyed observing others. I was struck by seeing my classmates take their first steps in love. I could film away the problems I had with love myself. While we were shooting the film, the most beautiful girl in the class fell in love with my best friend who was playing the lead role. When I turned seventeen we made a 16mm version of that film, which was shown on Flemish and Danish television. I read the film magazines I ordered from America, devoured books on film, scenario writing and editing techniques.

I took the entrance examination for the HRITCS twice and passed it twice. But I never enrolled in film school—it was too chaotic for me. It seemed amateurish. I wanted to be trained professionally. 'There's still a good film school in Poland, with Polanski,' I thought. But I didn't know any Polish.

The desire to be a film director has been inside me my whole life. It has become my baseline. Along with that great emotion: indignation. I started studying medicine, inspired by the motivation and courage of the doctors in Robert Altman's *MASH,* a movie about doctors in an American field hospital during the Korean war. I have had moments when I no longer knew which life I wanted, when I lost my way. After three years I quit medicine, I crashed. The doctors' authoritarian behaviour was suffocating me. I took my books about film and moved to France. There, I became a shepherd. 'I'm warm,' the head shepherd told me one day. I'll never forget those words: 'J'ai chaud,' and he fell down dead in the middle of the road. While the others went to the valley for help, I stayed behind with him, alone. I covered him with a plastic tarp that we used for protection against the rain. I had never seen a dead person before. I left the shepherds and became a lifeguard in a fashionable club full of film stars in Monaco. 'I don't want my legs to be exposed to the sun too much,' Grace Kelly told me. She would ask me to hold a towel in front of her legs every time she stood up from her deck chair. 'She doesn't think her legs are perfect enough to be seen,' her entourage told me. Ten years later she died in an accident on the winding road of La Turbie. When the director of the elite club offered me a future as a croupier in the casino, I went back to Belgium a year later. I didn't want that kind of life. But what kind of life I did want, that was still a big question. 'Maybe a film director after all?', I thought. But I couldn't get an exemption from physics classes, which put me off. So back to medicine. I wanted to finish what I had started. I was painfully aware of the injustice people suffered at the hands of the hubris of the medical world. Give people a uniform to wear and they'll believe they have power. It's something that has always bothered me. I can't stand authority. I have an endless aversion to people who create hierarchical differences through their behaviour. The differences between healthcare providers and doctors and patients, for instance. There are quite a few parallels to be drawn between hospitals and prisons. The word 'patient'

(3)

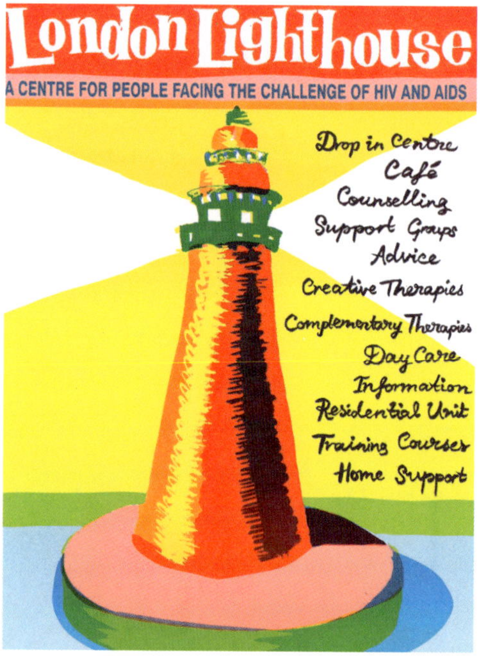

alone, that imposed sufferance, so full of patience. I hate that word. I have never wanted to call myself 'doctor'. I always say: 'I studied medicine'.

The do-gooder syndrome is something that stuck with me. I went on to study tropical medicine and then devoted myself to cancer research. I saw the doctors in the oncology department pass by the rooms of the incurably ill. Dying wasn't part of the doctor's therapeutic arsenal. To me, this was unjust. At the very least these people had the right to a conversation. But they were suffering, both psychologically and physically. This is why I started working in palliative care. Consideration for the dying. Psychological support. My colleagues looked at me as though I'd gone mad. Everyone is mortal, it's just that one is a bit further along in the process than the other. But the fact that someone is closer to the end doesn't mean they deserve to be patronised. People who are seriously ill often suffer more from the overbearing way they are treated by professionals than from their sickness. At the palliative and supportive day care centre TOPAZ, we wanted to create a space where people are equals, no matter how seriously or incurably ill. One has medical knowledge, the other has life experience. There is no hierarchical difference between healthcare providers, volunteers, artists and guests. Everyone is regarded as a human being, and no one as a sick person. We try to give as much meaning as possible to the time that remains. We don't want to make decisions over people's heads, we want to give people the means to rise above themselves. Many have narrowed down their lives to their illness alone. At TOPAZ,

(4)

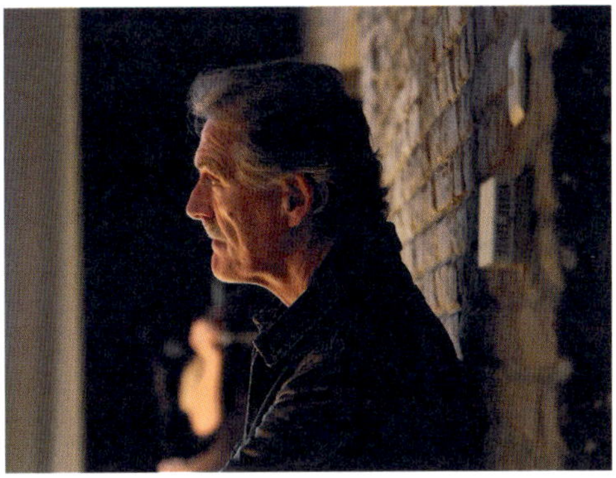

everyone reopens that life together. Living is about having a perspective, about seeing possibilities in the future. Becoming a film director is an idea I want to keep alive for as long as possible. And if I ever do it, I'll do it in the same way I work at TOPAZ now: trusting in every person's power and creativity, giving everyone free reign to do what they feel like doing and trying to work in the same direction together. Creating a broader and more open view on the world together. Actor-centric cinema. Not director-centric cinema, that I've never cared for.

This text is based on a text by Anna Luyten and was first published in Dutch in the book: '*And?*', Jorge León, VUB Press 2017

(1) Grace Kelly by Howell Conant
(2) Still from M.A.S.H.
(3) A lighthouse with two beams of light left and right; advertisement for services provided by the London Lighthouse centre for those with AIDS and HIV. Colour lithograph by Sophie Herxheimer, 1991, ©Wellcome Collection. CC BY-NC
(4) Wim Distelmans by DYOD

95

96

97

98

99

100

102

103

104

MAGIC HANDS

Handwork has traditionally been assigned to the private sphere, especially to women. For a long time, there was no place for it in the professional art world, where it was considered a form of occupational therapy, at best. Now, handwork or 'craft' is often appreciated, precisely because it makes those visible who would otherwise remain invisible. It turns norms and values on their head, as it implies cooperation over individualism and values process over product, time over money. In this chapter, old traditions and new practices are closely interwoven. Some years ago, journalist and researcher Hilde Bouchez travelled to Kyrgyzstan for her research on the value of handcrafting. She was intrigued by the carpet weaving practices being used by women in some nomadic tribes. It soon became clear how deeply their craft is intertwined with life. As a ritual, it has become the centre of the tribe's existence and beliefs. In a second contribution, art critic and curator Isabel Debaets talks with Ann Weckx and Naomi Kerkhove, two artists working in healthcare settings who give new meaning to handcrafting. Together with guests of the palliative and supportive day care centre TOPAZ, Ann Weckx created a large installation, made of plastic trash materials. She considers her 'Supermarché des Petits Bonheurs Instantanés' a homage to the beauty of handicrafts. Naomi Kerkhove is known for making crocheted tactile miniature worlds, in which the audience can completely immerse itself. Naomi Kerkhove is one of the resident artists in the IN/FINITY project at TOPAZ.

106

Kyrgyzstan had been on my list of places to visit for almost my entire life. In my head, it had become a thrilling movie, with scenes of women on horseback galloping over the endless steppe, their long hair blowing in the wind as they follow their flocks to new pastures; a glorious landscape as a backdrop, dotted with colourful yurts and populated by an austere people who still carry the grandeur of their pre-Soviet occupation past. In my romantic narrative, the spirit of Genghis Khan still wanders the steppes: the great version, not the one who committed wholesale massacres.

My daughter and I board a Russian plane to fly east.[1] Anyone who complains about Ryanair should try flying Aeroflot. A late night layover of four hours in Moscow rapidly shatters any idealistic images I may have had about this trip and I realise that I will only be able to understand Kyrgyzstan if I allow Russia its place in the story.

Bishkek, capital of Kyrgyzstan, is a desolate place, entirely built by the Soviet regime. Before the arrival of the Russians, Kyrgyzstan barely had masonry, let alone concrete structures. The nomadic people moved from place to place with their herds and possessions.

It is scorching hot and dusty in this valley surrounded by snow-capped mountains: add to this the old, badly maintained cars and it is a city that leaves the taste of kerosene and soot at the back of your throat.

So we are glad to head into the mountains towards the Naryn region. There we will have our first encounter with the country's felt-making women: the reason for our journey. I read somewhere that these women not only create blankets and rugs out of boiled wool but also whisper to their creations, and that they have been doing so for generations: what they are making are not objects but stories, lives and gifts. This reminds me of a piece of research from 1925 by the anthropologist Marcel Mauss that showed conclusively that gift-giving was an essential form of social bonding for ethnic groups in Polynesia en Melanesia.[2] But this trip is far from being any attempt at anthropological research. Instead, it was inspired by my curiosity about the tangibility of the whispering love of these felters, and perhaps even my incredulity.

If one were to describe rural Kyrgyzstan in one word, it would be 'rough'. Rough as the hair of the goats and sheep, of the deeply grooved faces of the shepherds and the hands of the women who spend their lives from dawn to dusk working to keep their children fed. The majority of the Kyrgyz live in primitive dwellings in isolated villages, or continue to live in felt yurts perched in inhospitable places high up in the mountains with views over a never-ending, empty landscape.

'Slow' is another word one could use to describe Kyrgyzstan: sitting on the backs of horses as they climb slopes that don't appear as steep as they are, or riding in minibuses along the roads that vanish into relentlessly monotonous landscapes. Waiting for what the day will bring, and that is often nothing at all.

It is a country of shepherds who endured Soviet oppression for too long and are now looking for new jobs that are less rough and slow than life in a yurt.

Impoverished Kyrgyz leave to find work cleaning toilets for a pittance for their distant neighbours, the rich Russians. The country is looking for ways to survive in a globalised world where Coca-Cola is sold in every village. In Kyrgyzstan, the Ministry of Health sends teams of nutritionists to all the villages to inform the residents that drinking Coca-Cola can be fatal. A nine-year-old boy recently dropped dead after drinking an entire bottle of it after a sporting event. The shift in only one generation from yak's milk to Coca-Cola has taken a heavy toll.

What seems to have remained unchanged is the tradition of felting by women, who have now moved down from the high plateaus to lower-lying villages. This is one of the few thriving crafts that are still practiced at home, and one that owes its survival to interest from the international market.

Although most of the women whom we visit are now in possession of a table and chairs, their homes and way of life still retain the atmosphere of a yurt, the latter of which is often relegated nowadays to the status of summer home.

Guljamal (60) grew up—like most people of her age—in the mountains. During the summer months, her entire family and their sheep, cows and horses would relocate to the high plateaus. It was only in the coldest months that they would live in the primitive houses of the valley. Before the Soviet era, thc Kyrgyz lived all year round in thick felt yurts, which became hard and water-resistant through the damp and the cold. The Russians brought 'progress' and scattered small, rudimentary villages with schools and hospitals across the country. The nomads turned into semi-nomads and most of them have now migrated to lowland towns and villages. As summer begins, the few remaining shepherds leave with their thousands of animals to spend four months in the mountains. Many families join the shepherds during the school holidays. The yurt has become synonymous with the caravan. The nomadic tradition continues, but in a modern, globalised form.

The making of shyrdaks and alakiizes, two types of felt carpet, used to be a daily activity for the women in the highlands. On the one hand, it helped to pass the time, on the other the carpets were essential for furnishing the yurts: but the main reason for felting was to create gifts for births, marriages and funerals. The floors of their homes and yurts are littered with a mosaic of rugs that have been collected over a lifetime: either made by themselves or received as gifts.

Guljamal shows us how she still makes alakiizes and shyrdaks, as gifts, but mainly as a way to make extra money. Today, she sells rugs primarily to tourists and foreign retailers through a NGO.

An alakiiz is a felt rug into which the colours and patterns have been pressed, whereas the coloured felt is sewn together to make a shyrdak. It is straightforward to make an alakiiz: all the women and children get involved.

Since it's raining, we retreat into a shed behind Guljamal's large house in a suburb just outside Kochkor. Her mother sits waiting on a stool while her daughter and granddaughter lay out the felt ready to make an alakiiz. Her great-grandchildren are playing outside and enter at regular intervals, impatient to start their assigned task.

Guljamal fetches a huge bundle of brown sheep's wool from the large, black rubbish bags that are stacked along the back wall of the shed, which she then carefully places on a large canvas sheet on the floor. Using slender willow sticks, the women rhythmically beat the wool. Guljamal explains how the dull thuds used to be audible throughout the valley and that women would recognise the rhythmic beating as a signal to come and help. This collective village activity is no longer done today, although it is a family enterprise. We sit on a bench quietly watching the women. They look very ordinary, the shed is likewise lacking in any exotic attractions, but the women make an impression on us. As though engaged in a ritual dance, they move around the wool, beating it in time with each other. A trance-like state comes over us as spectators: a sort of rhythmic silence that opens up our hearts.

Once the wool has been completely pulverised, the pieces are arranged in a square. This forms the base of the rug, on to which coloured wool shapes are laid. This appears to be a job reserved for Guljamal's daughter-in-law, who is very talented according to our hostess. When, later, they start making shyrdaks, it is once more the daughter-in-law who draws the designs on the felt. She has 'the gift'.

The work is carried out in silence, no one gives instructions, and yet slowly but surely a clear pattern emerges from what was originally a pile of unprocessed wool: the traditional kochkor (ram horns) bordered with the mountains of Kyrgyzstan. When the women are happy with the design, the rug is carefully rolled up in a reed mat, tied up and soaked with boiling water. A rope is wound around it and Guljamal uses it to slowly drag the rolled-up rug around while the children stamp on it as hard and fast as they can. There is laughter and this part of the making process seems to be literally child's play.

While the youngest generation has fun with the roll, Guljamal tells us how rug-making brings a family together. Daughters learn from their mothers and grandmothers. The making of shyrdaks and alakiizes has always been an enjoyable activity that brought women together to relax and at the same time to bequeath their best intentions to the rug. Furthermore, Guljamal explains, the role of the children is vital. The Kyrgyz believe that when children stamp on the roll, the colours become more vivid since the children are doing it with such delight. Their joy lights up the rugs.

Making rugs is a form of expressing love that brings the women closer to each other, but also—through invisible threads—to the people for whom the rug is being made. Positive thinking, which occurs naturally when making these rugs, is crucial to the creative process. The loose strands of wool are, as it were, united and held together by intentions of love, happiness, success, prosperity, etc.

For every rug in her house, Guljamal can recall when she made it and with what intentions, or from whom she received it and the emotions that were aroused. A shyrdak or an alakiiz are far more than functional objects designed to keep your feet warm: they are amulets with hidden scripts. Each symbol has a specific meaning, each fibre carries a positive intention.

After about one hour, the roll is opened. We can tell that this is an important moment. Everyone comes to stand around it and, as Guljamal explains afterwards, everyone wishes for it to be a beautiful rug that will bring prosperity, both to those who receive or buy it and to those who made it. Because the more the rug is adored, the more good things will come to us as the makers.

The rug is greeted with joy, then the children return to their game and the women resume work. They kneel in front of the rug and roll it back and forth. It seems like a prayer and, once again, there is this strange silence carried on the rhythmic movements. Guljamal tells us that men cannot be present during this part of the making process: it is the critical moment when the women get energy from the rug and the rug gets love from the women. But sometimes the magic doesn't work and the rug is ugly. According to Guljamal, that may be the result of one of the women having a negative thought or intention, or one of the makers being troubled, or it could even be because the person for whom the rug was made has a guilty secret.

A felter in another village tells me about the process of creating the pattern that when they draw the patterns, it isn't from something they have learned. The drawings come straight from the heart, from the soul. It's like writing a poem. If a woman doesn't have that feeling inside her, she can't draw a pattern. They are visions. Those who have this gift are nothing more than a sort of middleman, a medium who interprets universal love and literally cuts and sews it into the rug. 'That is the essence of making. That is the essence of our people: letting love flow into the closed circle of our world, even into the most mundane objects.'

Without realising it, she has summed up the very essence of my book.

This text was first published in the book 'A Wild Thing' by Hilde Bouchez, APE 2017.

1 This travelogue describes a trip undertaken in June 2014.

2 Mauss, M., The Gift: Forms and Functions of Exchange in Archaic Societies, Cohen & West LTD, 1966 (1950).

Embroidery: Naomi Kerkhove,
'Le Star' / 'The Star'

DE
STAR

Continuing our reflections on the relational aesthetics, the social and political engagement as well as the project- and process-based work that characterise the last decades, we notice that more and more artists are opting to work in the context of active life, in direct interaction with people or other actors in society. The most significant implication of these more relational forms of art is that they require the collaboration and involvement of others in order to come into being. The one-sided focus on the creation of artworks in the studio has been replaced by an emphasis on the creation of the conditions that enable 'happenings' with people in the here and now, or that set work- and social processes in motion among participants. Within this broad spectrum of participatory practices, we also find the more recent co-creative practices, which deeply engage with the current technological revolution in society, its far-reaching digitalisation and robotisation.

Individual artist studios are making way for co-creation platforms and workspaces, where people collaborate in workshops, taking on the role of active participants, users or co-creators. Here, they apply collaborative and working models, which in many cases function primarily as 'tools' to offer the participants experiences and insights. In these artistic practices, the created objects also have a different status. They often serve as a means of communication, their main purpose being to enable the working process.

We also see this tendency translated in the work of Ann Weckx and Naomi Kerkhove, two artists who embarked on an artistic project centred on handicrafts at the palliative and supportive day care centre TOPAZ (Belgium). We asked Ann and Naomi what it means to them, as artists, to work not individually, but in collaboration with other people, 'outside' of the familiar studio and, in their case, in a care centre. Artists who develop artistic practices within the care sector and involve the guests (patients) in these, often take on a humble, serving attitude. In the course of our conversation I learn that, from the outset, they ask themselves: how can I address the needs of the other? For Ann Weckx, this deeply empathetic attitude is essential if you want to realise anything in this sector. 'As an artist, when you enter TOPAZ, you have to temporarily stop being an artist, and at first simply be a person among other people. You need time to realise where you've arrived. The more time you take, the more you can organically insert yourself as an artist into the functioning of the day centre and the lives of the people in it. After that, you can slowly start getting to work.' Naomi Kerkhove adds: 'When you enter TOPAZ, you first have to let go of yourself and your plans, as it were. You have to get to know the people and the reality of the day centre, which changes from day to day: different guests, different volunteers, etc. You're confronted with people who have all kinds of disabilities. Some have a very limited tactile ability, others have a limited mobility. Some gravitate toward fixed habits, whereas others don't at all.'

A question that quickly arises is how to deal with this process-based element, when more emphasis is placed on the process than on the created art object and the social process itself becomes a form of art. Naomi sees the embroidery work she does in her artistic practice at TOPAZ as a means of communication rather than as an 'artwork'. 'By creating something in the presence of the guests, or by working on something with concentration, you trigger things within them. Because you're working on art and not on healthcare, you preserve your freedom and you're able to have a straightforward conversation. And this is precisely what is of crucial importance to the guests.' Ann also affirms the value of the creative process: 'When the guests are drawing with Naomi or myself, they suddenly lose their sense of time, which is amazing. Without our intending to do art therapy, our activities may sometimes have a therapeutic effect. What I find so interesting in this is the smallness of the thing itself. A small gesture can have a huge impact on someone at a specific moment. Often, what occurs is a kind of exchange that sets something in motion for both people. We try to integrate these forms of dialogue or interaction between people into our work.'

It soon becomes clear that the practices Naomi and Ann have introduced at TOPAZ require a significant amount of time to realise. They focus on a lot of direct contact between people and start a process of dialogue within the group. To Naomi, it's important, in our fast-moving world—which can easily drag you along with it—to make time, on occasion, for this kind of deep and direct fundamental contact with people. 'We risk having less and less time for this kind of contact, which means we risk losing something. In fact, we are losing our humanity. I want to show this through my work, that's why everything I do starts from this direct dialogue with the guests at TOPAZ.' For Ann, the beauty of handcrafting lies in the fact that it develops from a drawn-out process. 'Time is important', she says, showing us a detail from an installation she made. 'You see, this flower is made from plastic bags that had texts on them. At a certain point, even these materials yield their poetry, which is a beautiful thing to experience. Handcrafting is a game, but one without a winner or a loser. For example, I'm making a flower and think to myself: if I were to use red twice and blue four times, how would my flower change? It's a game you can continually keep playing with yourself. In the film 'De handen van mijn vrienden' (the hands of my friends) (2018), I also tried to capture how handcrafting consists of one action following another. You start with one stitch and watch the work literally grow into something large as you're working.'

Ultimately, Ann also sees the process-based element of handcrafting as a form of self-care. 'When I was working intensively on my tapestries for a time, I would come out of my studio every day feeling reborn. I noticed that handcrafting is necessary for my own survival process. It's something that allows me to give a shape to my own loneliness and to break through it. I've also observed that this kind of handcrafting acquires much more meaning within the context of TOPAZ. I've noticed that, in times of loneliness, many people come back to certain everyday, manual activities, like cooking for yourself, gardening in your own garden, making your own clothes. We see the same thing at TOPAZ. The guests feel the urge to recreate that connection between head and hands. The head is freed by working with the hands, and what is incredible about it is that it really works. This is something that hasn't changed over the centuries, except that we've lost the art of craftsmanship. Working with your hands and 'making-together' isn't only something enjoyable that makes you feel strong. It also creates a 'being-together' between different people, in a situation that is absolutely not threatening and in a time and space you can choose for yourself. It's a kind of social space in which stories are told and, through this, connections are formed.'

It therefore appears that the value of handcrafting lies, on one hand, in the small gestures, the meditative techniques that bring calm and stillness, placing you in a different space and bringing you to the essence of your being and, on the other hand, in the creation of that social space that works outwards, forges connections, seeks expansion and kinship. The question that many would pose here is to what extent this value is an artistic value, and whether we wouldn't rather classify handcrafting in the care sector as 'occupational therapy'.

Yet Ann and Naomi's long-term handcrafting projects go far beyond occupational therapy. Its boundaries are surpassed in the working process—within the mental and social space specifically created by the artists—though this is difficult to measure. Where this can be measured is in the material outcome of the work. Even though, as indicated above, both projects focus more on the process than on the artwork resulting from it, we cannot neglect the visual-aesthetic quality of the material work that has been created.

Thus far, Naomi has maintained control over the material aspect/handcrafting in her project, allowing her embroidery work to fully maintain her artistic signature. This is different in the case of Ann's installation 'Le Supermarché des Petits Bonheurs Instantanés', as the final result was a material creation emerging from a collaborative effort. Still, the aesthetic quality of this work is without a doubt due to the artistic input of the guiding artist. She plays an essential role as a gently directing, mediating force in the co-creation process, and as a guardian of both this process and the aesthetic quality of the material end result.

The guests at TOPAZ have indicated their abilities and skills. It is to the artist's credit that she was able to engage with these and adapt the working process accordingly, which isn't to say that she simply left the guests without any guidance. At every moment of the process, she had a sort of overarching plan in mind and knew where she wanted to go with the participants, which allowed her to adjust the project when necessary. As a result, the material work created by the group could be effortlessly inscribed into Ann's artistic signature or imagery. As the guiding artist, she consistently acts from within a well-defined artistic framework: her conceptual vision. Through this approach, the handcrafted work transcends the domain of pure ‘craft’.

Another reason why Ann and Naomi fit well within the care sector is that both artists apply accessible artistic techniques and have a ‘rough’ way of working, meaning that guests with limited mobility or tactility are also welcome to participate actively and open themselves up to the unexpected.

Both artists see value in the guests’ limited artistic knowledge and bounded abilities. Naomi argues that sometimes, we have to let go of what we know in order to learn or to reach something new. ‘Art can be a free pass, a journey during which to be or to do, to move or stand still.’ Ann adds: ‘and to be allowed to fail, something that is no longer allowed or accepted in our society. Yet we have the right to make something that may be worthless according to others. That’s what I love. Handcrafting allows us to keep coming up with new solutions. It allows us to remain children and keep discovering forever.’

Embroidery: Naomi Kerkhove,
‘Stil’ / ‘Quiet’

Following pages:
still from ‘the hands of my friends’
by Ann Weckx/Jan Michiels

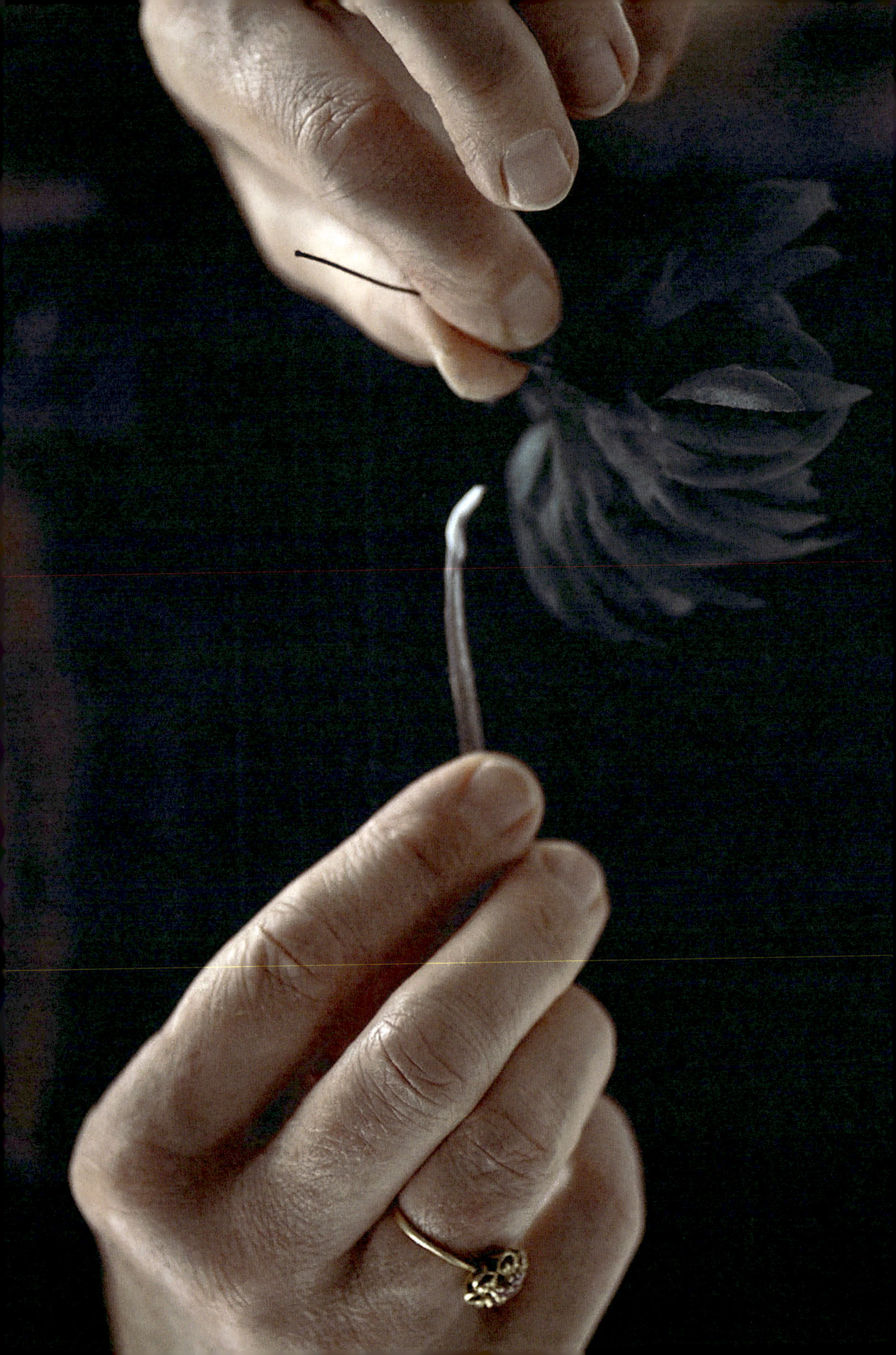

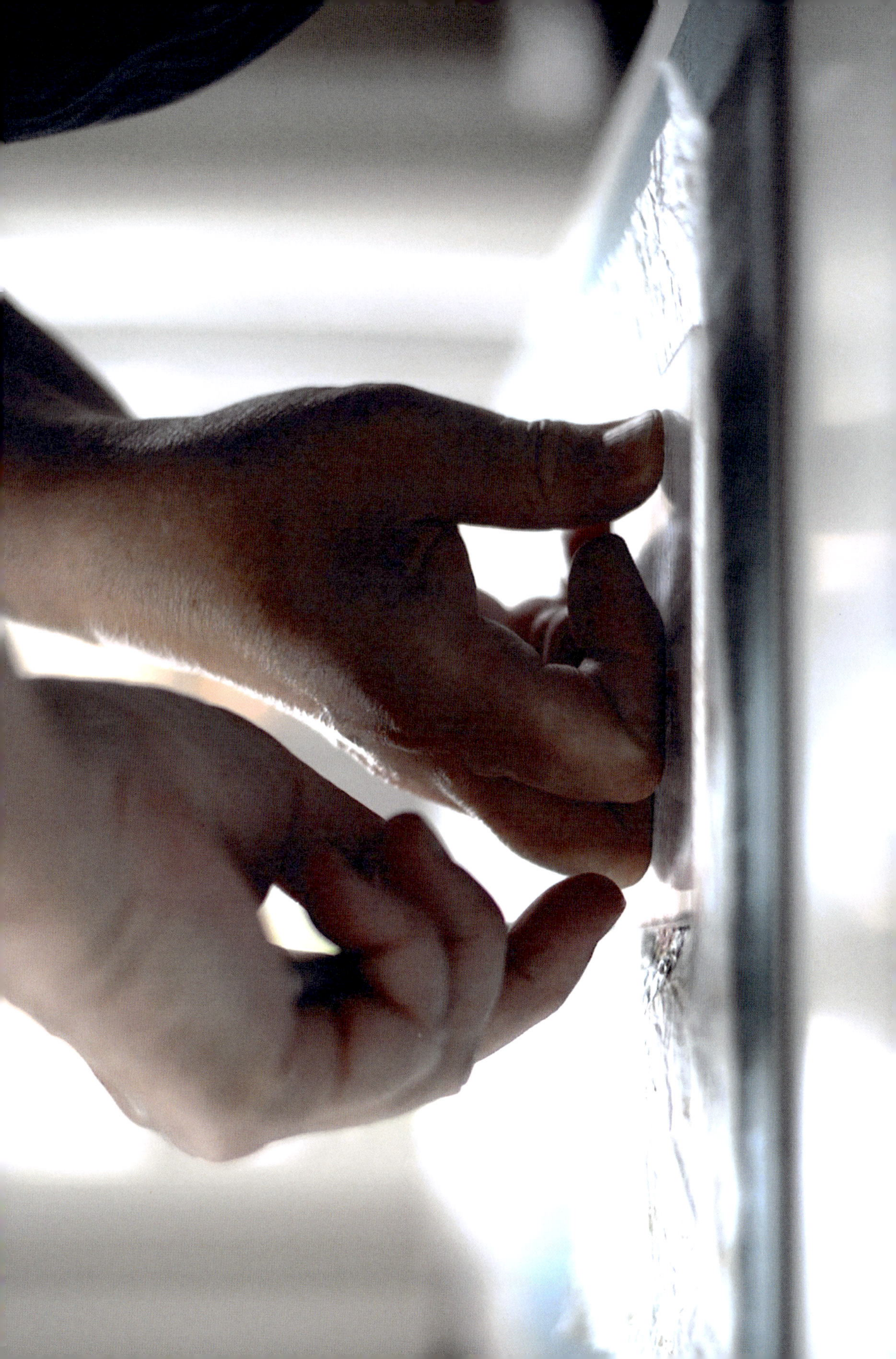

120

FORGET / REMEMBER / IMAGINE

121

When our health fails us, our world is often reduced. We are left with no choice but to live in the present. Plans and dreams for the future are put on hold, and likewise our past can become irrelevant. In such a situation, our imagination can become a meaningful and powerful force in our existence. Where memories disappear, our imagination can step in to (re)create them. Where our body ties us to our bed, our mind can take us anywhere we want to go. If we're stuck in a story, our imagination can help us break out. The power of our imagination is what drives us as creative beings. Artists prove to be great partners in this process of imagination, both by creatively imagining themselves what others fail to imagine, or by functioning as a catalyst for someone else's imagination.

In her work, Emi Kodama uses everyday objects like paper, a pencil, a little stone from the backyard or a walnut to take you on a journey into your own imagination. She weaves stories from your dreams and thoughts, creating very personal pieces of poetry.

It begins at the tip of your pencil
Emi Kodama

122

Mountains are something I experience mainly in my memory and imagination now that I live in Ghent, Belgium. The gray-blues and the blue-greens of Canada's west coast. I think of my inner world as a space that I can explore and expand. One way I do this is by hiking through landscapes that I remember, which makes their fuzzy edges sharpen and come into focus as I spend time there. But I'm aware that my experience and creativity have their limits, so I get out into the wilderness from time to time to fuel my imagination.

My work has a dual purpose: I write stories as a way to wander places I can't physically go, and I develop them into performances to share my memories and imaginings with others.

People aren't used to spending extended periods of time in their inner worlds. There isn't much of an opportunity for it in daily life. My performances guide people into their imaginations through storytelling. When people listen to stories, they usually shut out their surroundings to concentrate on the world that the narratives generate inside them. But we are bodies in space, and I've been exploring the ways that the physical world can add to the story and connect to their inner worlds. In my work, I engage the audience's senses as they listen to a story while drawing, interacting with objects, or sitting in a specific setting.

The stories aren't only created by me, but also by the listeners. I merely suggest, and they actively use their imaginations. For example, a walnut tree in a story is visualized slightly differently by each person. Through this experience, I'd like people to appreciate how vibrant their inner worlds are.

In the one-on-one performance 'It begins at the tip of your pencil', the guest closes their eyes and draws what they see with their mind's eye as they listen to the story I tell. Their pencil point follows the contours of the scene in their imagination. Drawing connects their body to their inner world and helps them concentrate on what they imagine.

Put on the blindfold. Run your hand over the surface of the paper. Feel its edges. Pick up the pencil.

Draw a vertical rectangle at the bottom of the page.

Imagine standing in front of it. It is a wooden door. The surface has a rough texture that you run your hand over. Follow the grain of the wood with your pencil. What could be behind the door? Draw a small circle waist-high. It's a doorknob.

When you turn it and push it open, a forest appears. You step through the doorway, and the temperature changes. Everywhere you look, the light is a pale green.

Focus on the closest tree. Walk towards it. When you look up, the leaves block out the sky. Think about how long it has been growing.

Choose a part of the tree that seems easiest to climb and draw it. Follow the branches with your pencil, each one higher than the last. Stop and touch a leaf. Turn it over and look at the details on its underside. A caterpillar has eaten a shape out of it. What does it remind you of? Trace its outline.

When you look down, the flowers on the ground are a field of colour. Sketch the pattern that the breeze makes through them.

As you continue climbing, you realize there is someone sitting on a branch above. From the shape of the figure, you have a vague idea of who it is. You climb quickly to check. Yes, it is who you thought it was.

'What are you doing here?' you ask.

'Waiting for you.'

One side of their face is in shadow, but both their eyes are shining. Follow the shape of their face with your pencil. Trace the slope of their shoulders and the folds in their clothes. You've seen them many times before—both in person and in photographs. Think of all the different ways that you have seen them. This may not even be the first time you've been up in a tree together. You sit next to them on the branch and swing your legs. You are surrounded by birds.

'I have something for you.' They dig into their pocket and pull out a shell. 'I found it on the beach.' It is warm and smooth in your palm and appears to glow in the light.

'Thank you.'

Turn the shell over in your hand and go over its patterns with your pencil.

It is about the size of your ear. You hold it close and listen.

Once, underwater, the two of you held your breaths for as long as you could. It must have been cold, but you don't remember anymore. You remember how your hair felt like a cloud around your head and how theirs looked like one. Their arms, tinted blue-green, moved in slow motion.

You pressed your knees against your chest and did one somersault and then another. The world spun, the sun first above, then below, then above again.

When you laughed, a stream of bubbles escaped your lips. They pointed at you gleefully, and you both swam to the surface.

All the swims you'd ever taken seemed to stretch behind you. Fast, slow, deep, shallow, clear, murky, with and without this person. They shouted as you broke through the water, and you gulped in a chestful of air, squinting in the clean, sharp light.

You put the shell in your pocket. When you look up, you notice that you can see the sky. It's a soft blue. Draw the space between the leaves.

'Have you been to the top?' you ask.

'Not yet.'

'Oh, what are we waiting for?'

As you reach the highest branch, the air changes. You stand tall, and there are trees as far as the eye can see. You are in a sea of treetops swaying in the wind, rolling, rippling. You are anchored in the middle of the forest. Layers of green absorb the light and fade to blue in the distance. You are close to the sky. When you turn your head, you catch the scent of salt water, and you realize the ocean isn't far away.

'I dreamed that we set sail for an unexplored island,' you say.

'Did we find it?'

'I woke up before we made it.'

'Well, I never thought this is where we'd end up.'

You both hold onto the trunk and forget how far you've come.

Now put down your pencil.

Remember the feeling of standing at the top of a forest.

Images: 'It begins at the tip of your pencil', photographed by Paul McGee

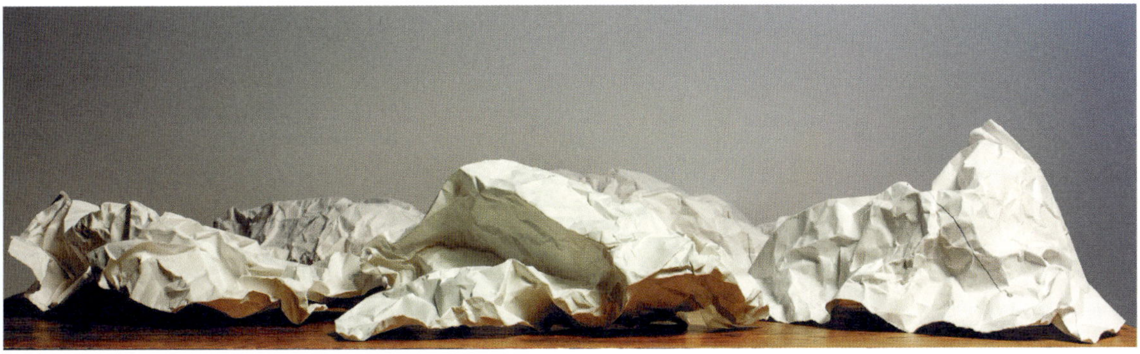

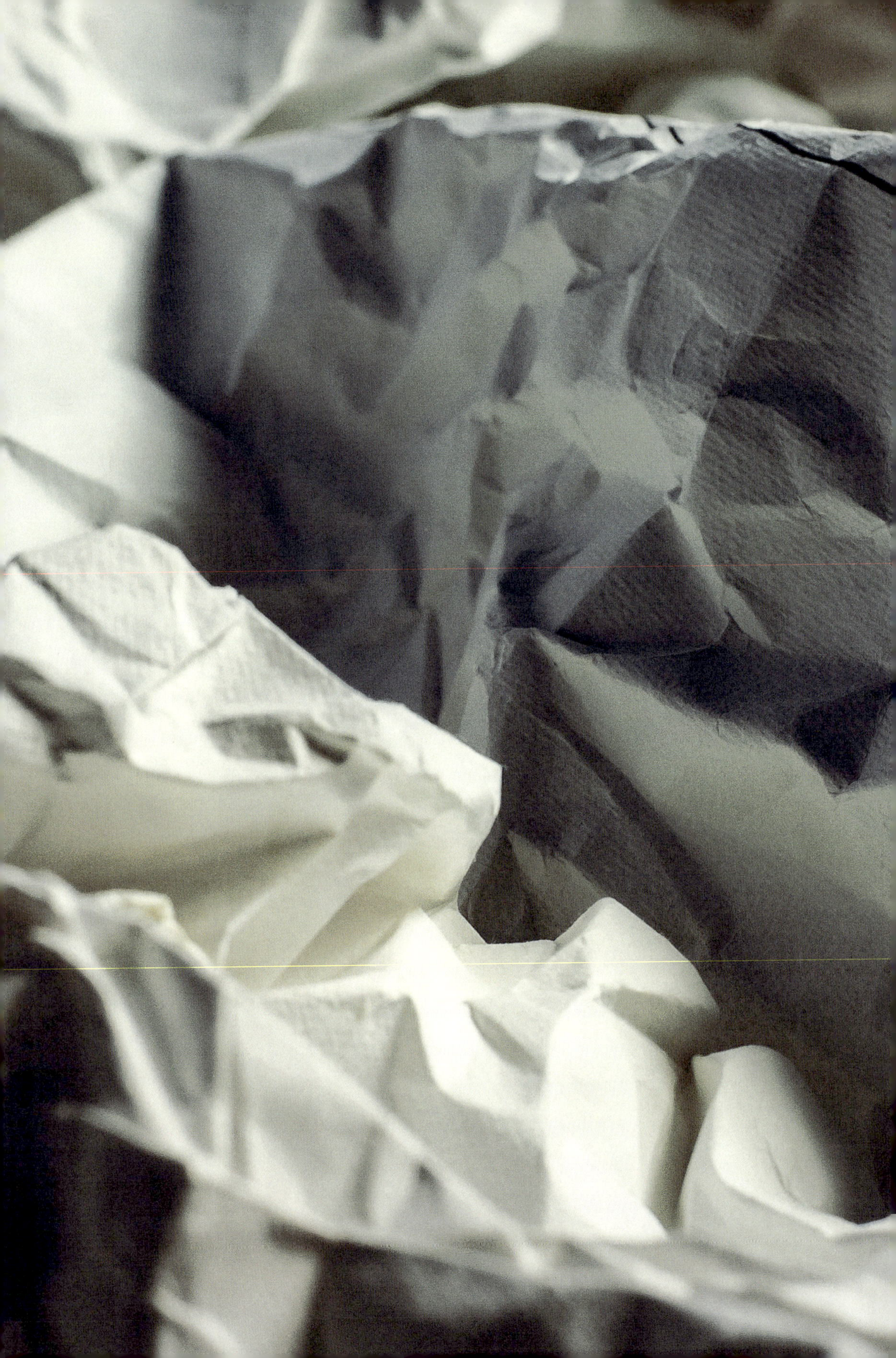

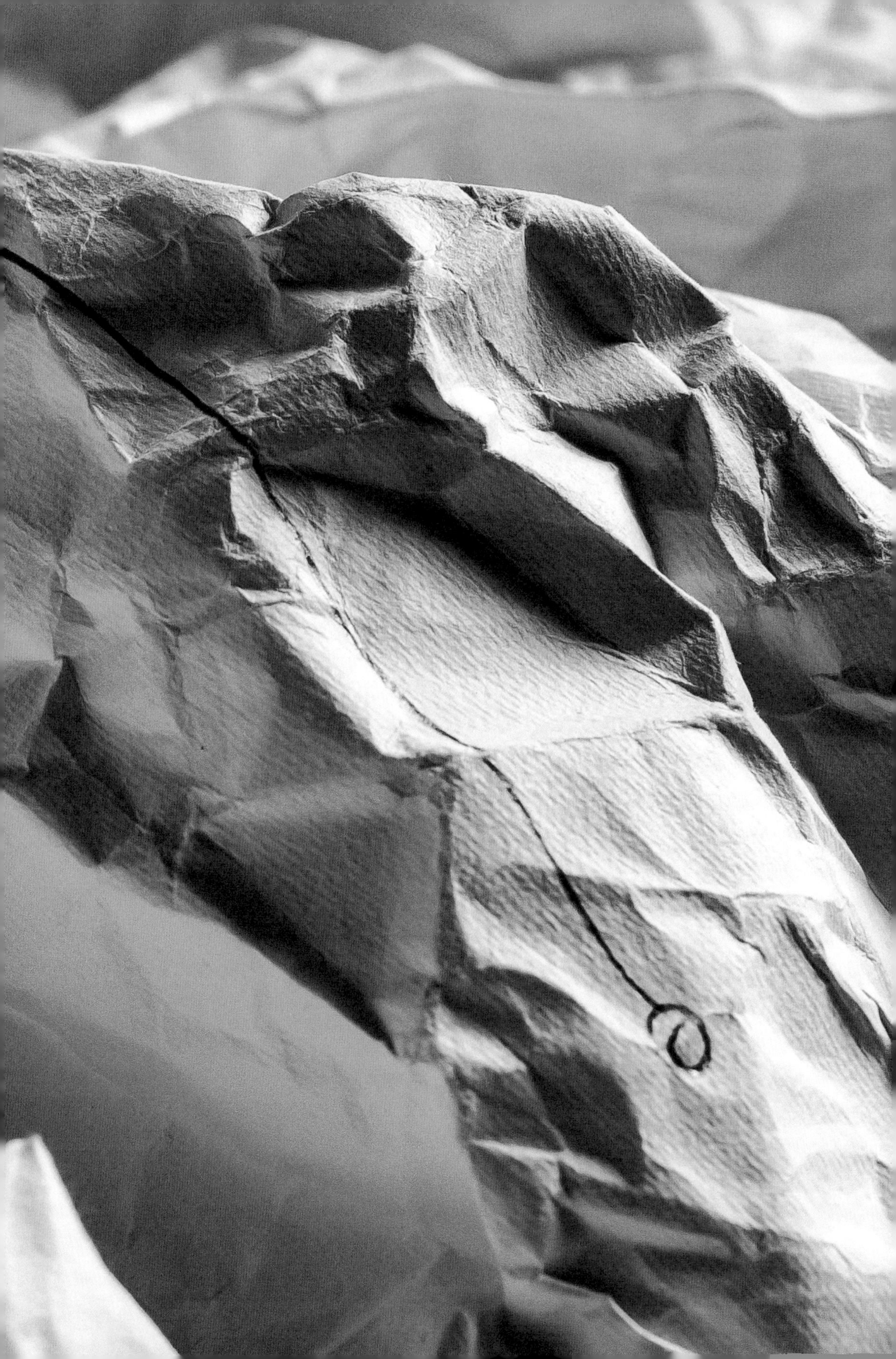

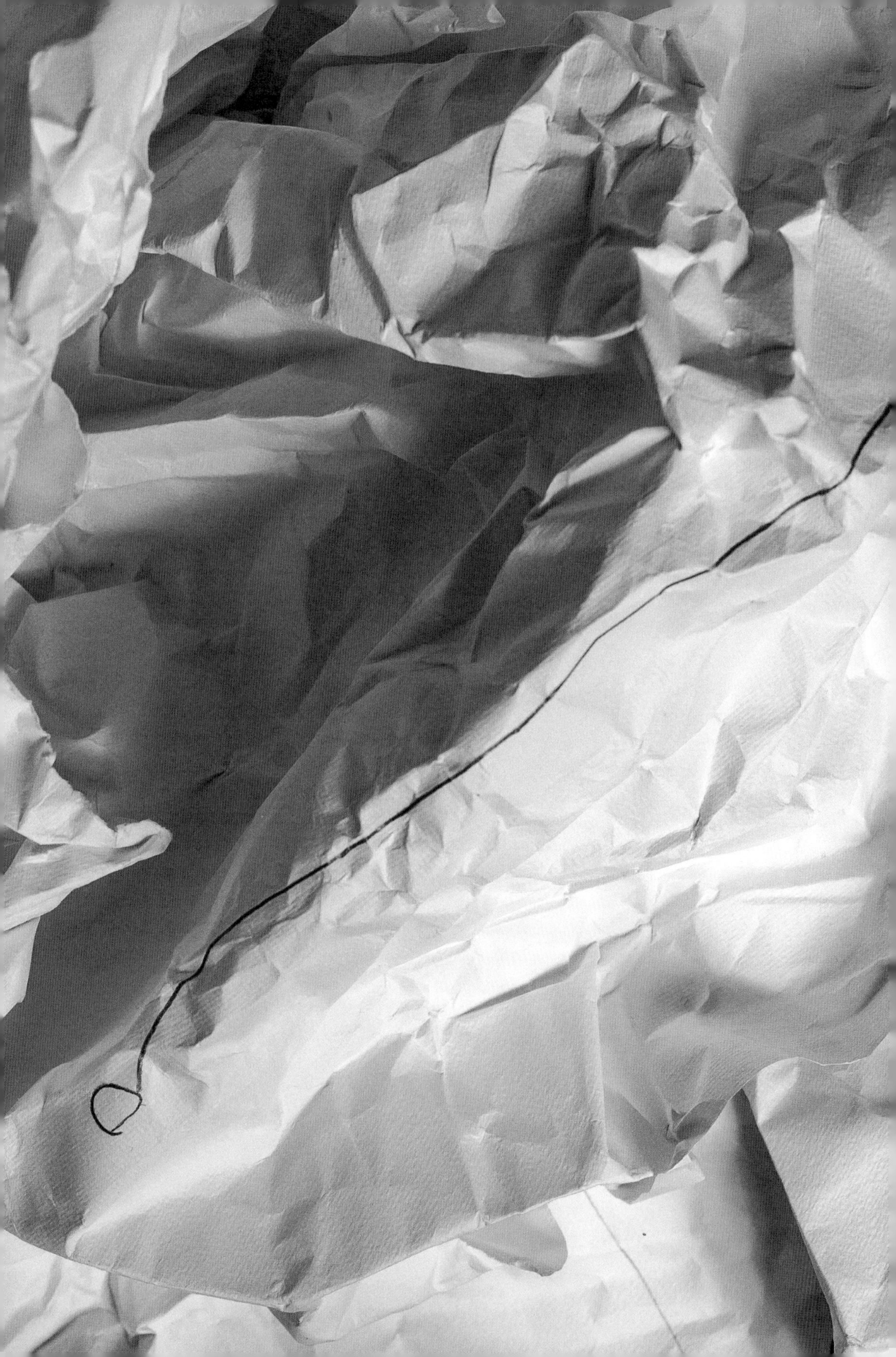

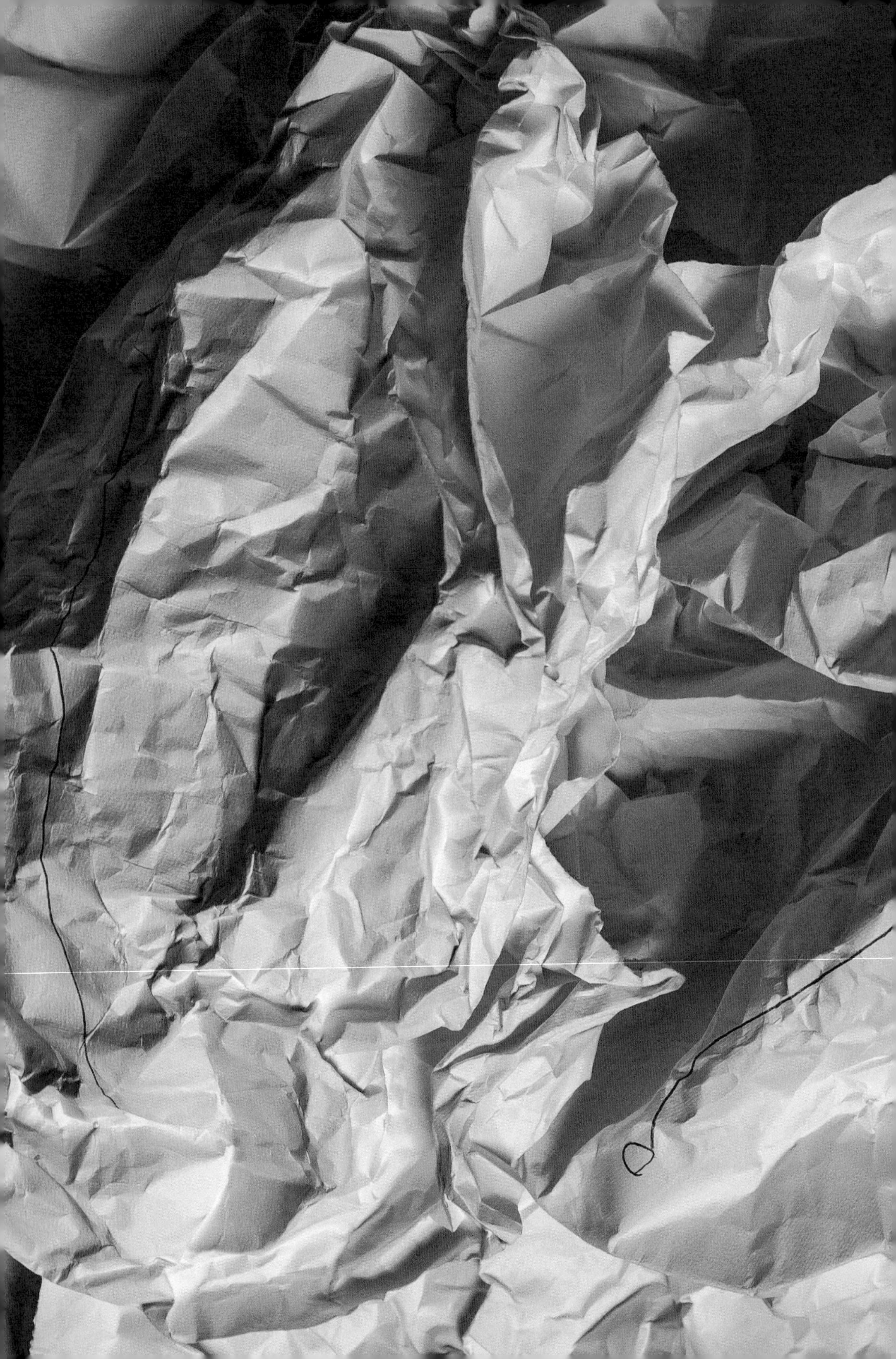

e

132

133

135

136

SHAPING IDENTITIES

137

More than anything, art (both in its creation by an artist and its experience by an audience) is an extension of our personal feelings, ideas and beliefs. It reflects upon and tries to answer some of our most fundamental existential questions. In various art-health collaborations, we were also able to see how art functioned as a medium for self-reflection and self-growth. We could see this working in both directions. On one hand, patients came to new insights and felt enriched by participating in these art projects. On the other hand, the artists also often told us that working in this healthcare context, where existential questions are never far away, made them question their own work and their identity as an artist.

The collective 'Oracle' (Caroline Daish, Justine Maxelon, Michel Yang) even took this a step further with their artistic practice. Together, these three artists create an improvisation practice where body, voice, identity and participation meet: a public, emancipatory and shareable act that involves individuality in a communal setting. In the next pages, they explain how such a practice came into being, and how the context of the TOPAZ palliative and supportive day care centre affected themselves and their work, and vice versa.

How Oracle Began
Caroline Daish, Justine Maxelon &
Michel Yang

138

1.

It began. That's it. How necessary is it to think about the real circumstances. I guess Mars was having a little twinkle blinkle with Jupiter, which angered Neptune to blow up in tears, which made Brussels a rather rainy place in November. Then snowy. To keep us warm we thought of action. Each of us due to different reasons, but each of us, meaning M and me, with the need to do it with C. So we did it with C and that's how we three met. Do you want to enlargen your vision of dance?

Three women got together in a borrowed free studio that doesn't exist anymore. They began sharing voice and practicing together. They agreed on some form and played together. It was winter. It was quite cold in the studio. There was no heating in the building. They wore many jumpers and layers. They were excited and pleased to be together. They didn't know each other that well. They had never all worked together before. They were feeling around and trying things out. One of them said she would lead the tasks. She had been asking her to try some stuff for some time. He happened to call her to do the same. But it was his first time. He was sick. She played ukulele. Their common friend brought the three together. And they began. They began in a space the common friend happened to have temporary use of, an artist squat. Rooms & spaces full of different artists squatting their ateliers, working space.

2.

She wasn't in shock. It was in her lungs. Breath. Inhale. Exhale. How else can she reach it? Touch it? Move it? Get closer to it? She called a friend. Would you like to get together to do some voice work or something? Yes, singing could be good. She wanted her body, her lungs to tremble. To move the molecules. To let her cells know she was there. She existed. That it was not alone. We'd do this together.

Frustration, Sadness, need for community. Illness, loss of belief. First you go down until you see the light coming up again. Oracle began as a light through difficult times. M was just diagnosed, C and me being rather frustrated with the ordinary way of how art is produced and the demand for an institutional way of working. Oracle came into being to shed some light into our misty brains, show new perspectives to work, form community around an art practice.

One woman had discovered that she had something growing in her lung but even before this she had asked if the other woman could explore/practice voice together. 'I want to do more vocal work. Can you do that with me?' Another woman joined. And actually I think that it was the young woman that put the idea of putting a form onto what they were doing. There was suspension, unknown. Time seemed to have stopped as they found out that the woman was sick.

3.

You know what? I don't know. But what I know is, that it is the best thing that happened to me in the last three years. Oracle became Home. Oracle became Hope. When we met the Oracle, we didn't know that we met the Oracle. We were walking in wonderland without realizing it for quite some time. We met something very strong, that's clear, otherwise we probably wouldn't have stayed connected artistically in all our differences. Oracle was the beginning, now the web is more complex.

I was excited to work and play with J and M. Such an unusual couple. They didn't know each other before. I think we were all looking for answers or openings, definitely beginnings and research. Playing—serious playing with who we are and who are these other people? Looking for alternative ways and answers to working with oneself, our bodies in a different way. And voice brings body and psychology together. It puts one on the spot, in the moment. The voice is idiosyncratic.

She was sitting at home. Writing. Knitting. Her son had just arrived. Time to get him a snack. She pulled out the chocolate cake that she had just baked. Gluten free. The phone beeps. It was J asking whey they could meet to play the ukulele and sing together. She realized she hadn't told J about the temporary access to a studio. Now would be perfect to practice this stuff there. She turns on the water kettle.

4.

Imagine. It began with imagining. Imagining that things can be different. Work different. Life different. It began with differences, coming together in harmonic disharmony. (From A to B on a mountaintop). It began with belief. A belief in vocalizing together, a belief in the healing power of doing things together. One of the first questions was: How to be yourself in community? It articulates with a desire. Oracle began with a desire. The need, the desire to reach inside one's voice but in the company of another. To use the body differently to enter the twilight zone of being inside of oneself and also outside and with others at the same time. To voice and not necessarily sing. To improvise. To use the voice as a physical manifestation or activity of oneself. To find out more about oneself. To have the freedom to move inside one's voice within a guided and protected form, well at least a form that allows free falling and catching, looking inside and outside.

The email flashed through her mind. She thought about last night. Her friend hadn't been drinking. But as if she was drunk, she had been non-stop. Her energy was moving her non-stop vortexing into her story. The sickness, the caring and not caring about finality. How is she now? Yes, she'll ask her to join her and J. Why not join?

5.

A carpeted floor in a building that is not existing anymore. C being the interface for this meeting.
A peeing position. (Strange, I'm so bad with peeing in a jar.) A peeing position. Three blind mice, see how they sing, see how they pee.
A carpeted floor in a building that is not anymore. C being the interface.
We meet. We sing. I'm wearing the same jumper as on the first day we met. The peeing-dog-jumper.
A carpeted floor that is not anymore.
Looking for answers that have never been proposed before. Hoping to have something from the future.
Reading the air, the environment and the future from this time, now, which is already the past. We strived to test, to take time, gently with two others. We wanted faith. We wanted to build faith in the body, voice, self, time, space, art, life, friendship, ridiculousness. We were looking for connection, fun and some healing time.
It as a dark and stormy night. J and C were warm & cozy inside by the fire drinking tea. The Auberge de Pecheurs offered a nit Hot Toddy. How could they refuse? The doorbell rang. Boris, the butler, led in the new arrival. A dark haired woman dressed in a long gown. Hair wet from the storm plastered to her face. Face white from cold.
'I have a cough,' she said.

Photos: Rasa Alksnyte

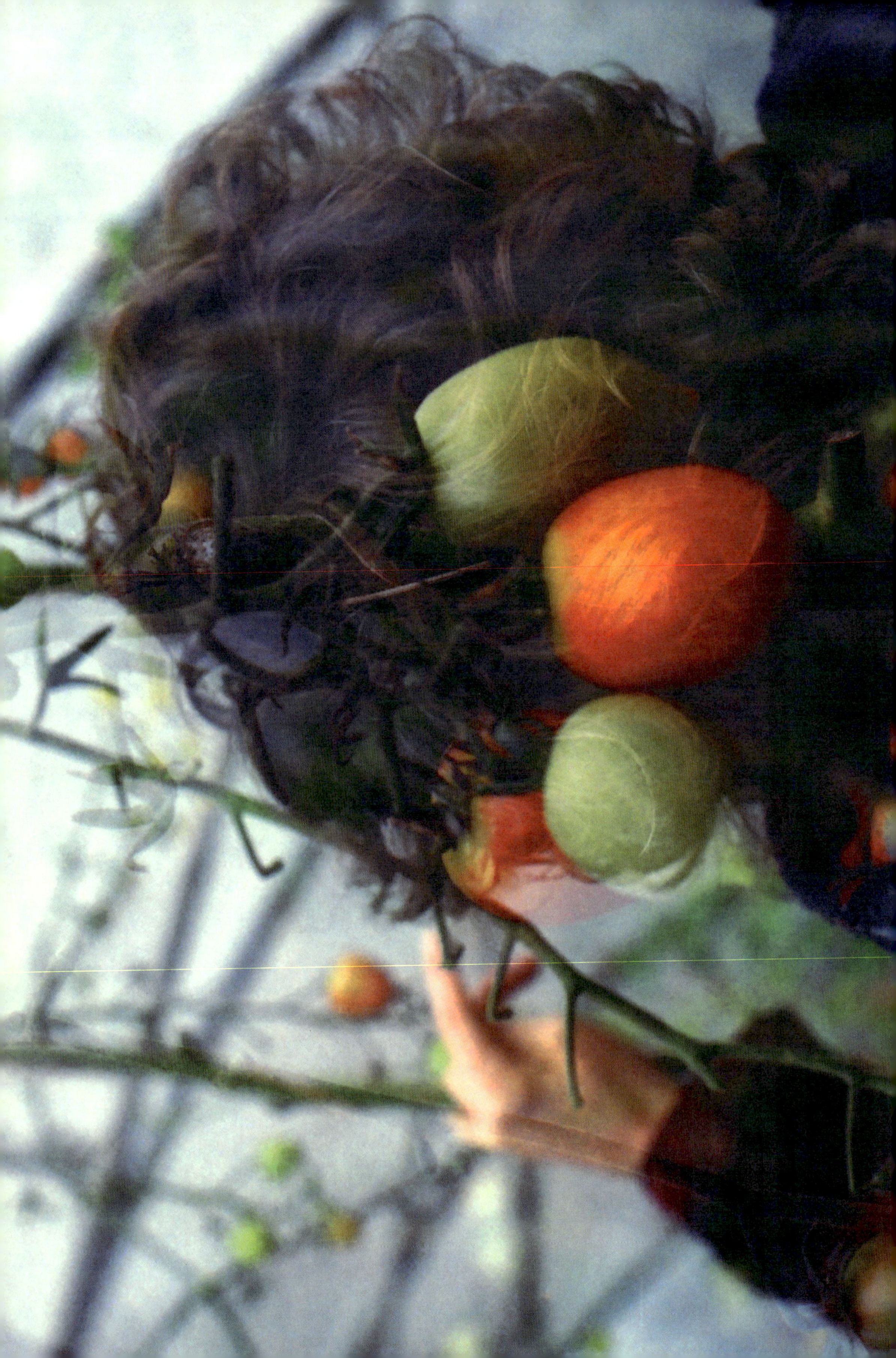

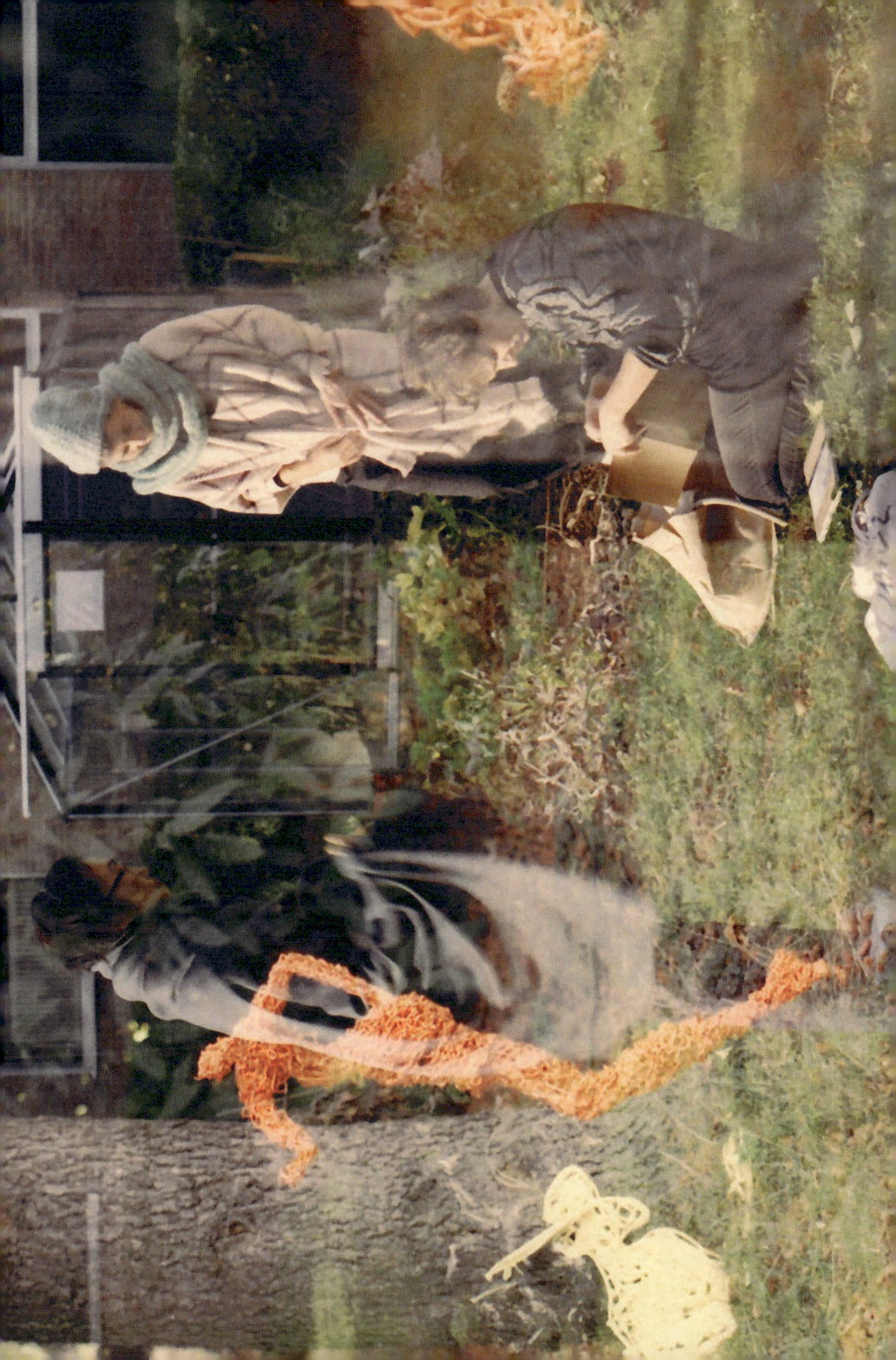

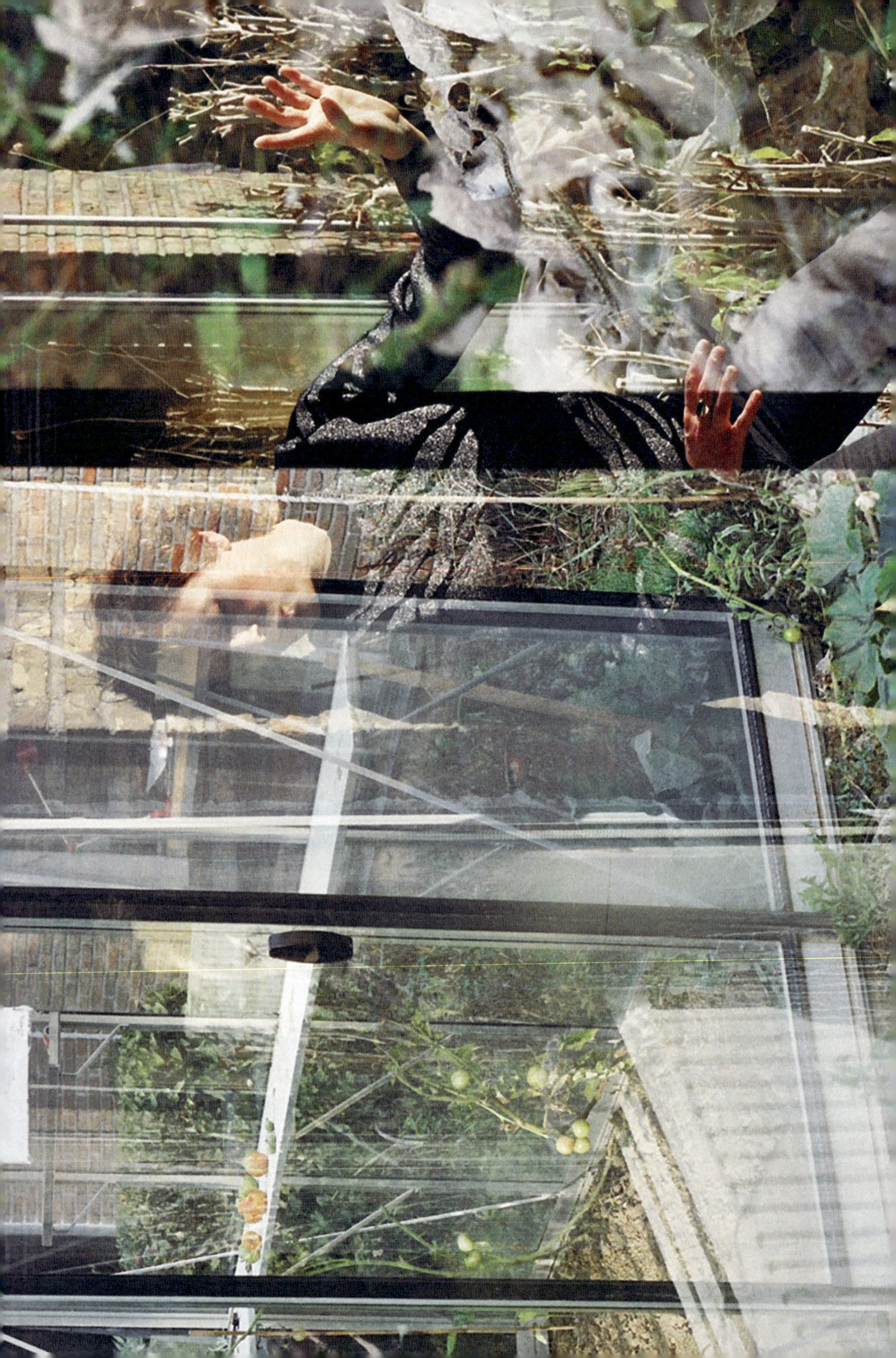

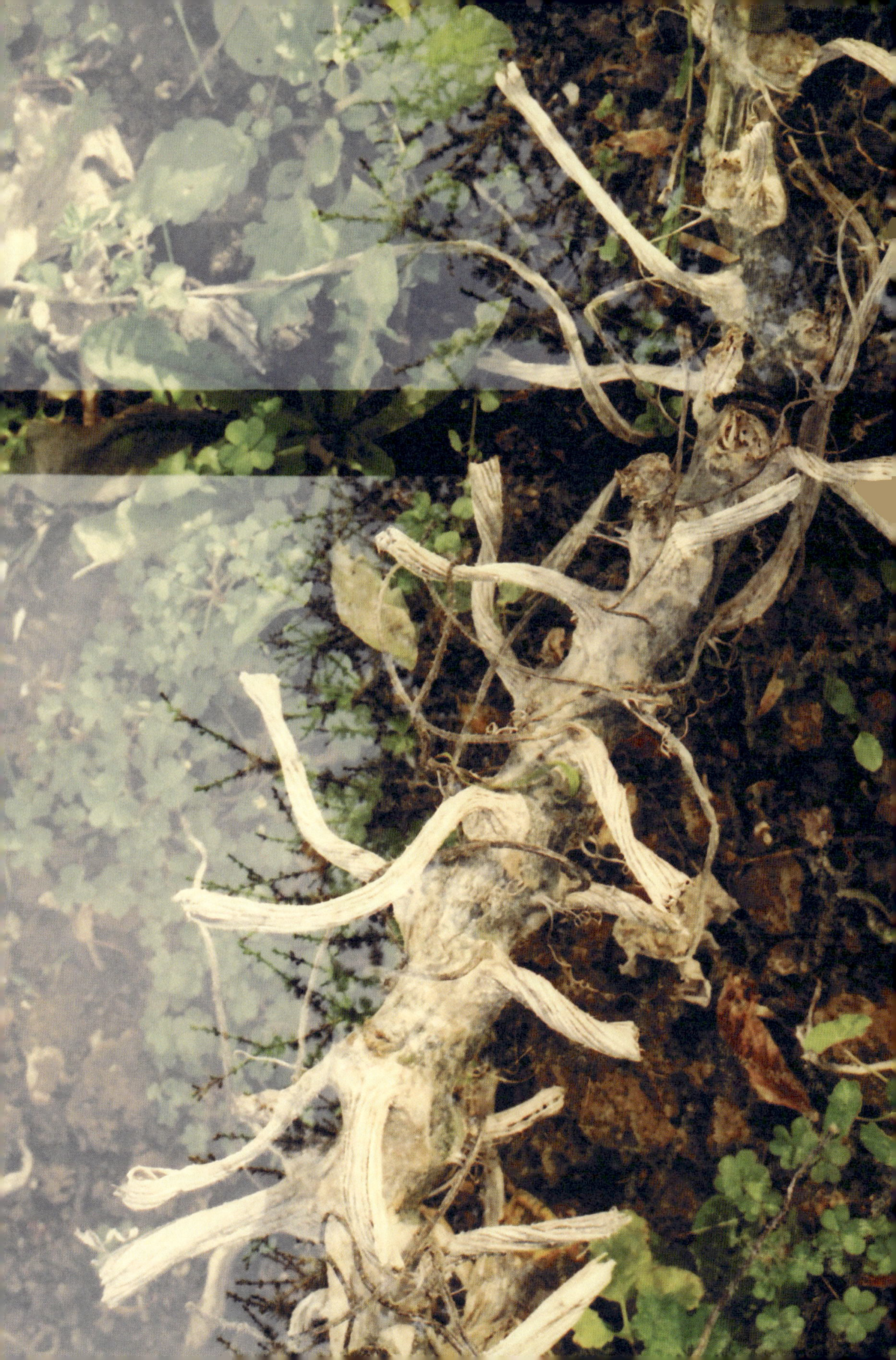

20 November 2018

A walk through a forest, soft rattling around, calm and soft interactions between the inhabitants of the space. A festive atmosphere. It feels like family. Small chatters, loving punches, necking each other. But all coming from a place of acceptance. Acceptance of sharing space and time with each other. And where are we?

Where am I? Hard to tell. A bit lost, making me remain sitting on one spot and allowing for the things to happen. My ass is rooted on the chair. I'm here, available.

Who are you all? I know why you all are here, i get little glimpses of your stories and still everyone remains a mystery. A meeting without the over-presence of past. Past is there, but looking from a more distant corner in the room.

One more day.

Just another day.

Closed eyes. Soundscape scoring. Bringing me here & present. Under the table channeling the soundscape of conversations, chatter, rummy tiles, French, Dutch, mumbles and J's music. No. Don't go away to the halls or toilets. They may be in between spaces, but the in-between-ness that you wish to embrace is in yourself. It's here at the clarity of the table. I am practicing, listening, vocal-channeling, using scoring as a supportive tool. Listen to the sea & sounds & layers. Being in-between the layers, between the tones, pitches, comments, words, a blur of layers, grasping to nothing. Not a word, not a voice, not a source. Like a baby just born, unable to distinguish between sounds borders, simply swimming in the sea of sounds.

23 October 2018

If I was to describe the air here... the unseen waves, the ultrasonic waves... what would that be? Strident Dutch to a hard of hearing and hushed tones. Like a high frequency fog in the air and disturbed every now and then. I get distracted. I try to gauge the day when I arrive. What is today? I think the walking in the open air is what happens to me. ABBA. 'Take a chance on me'. I can remember the words. Ideas for today. I on I's. Soundbath. Of course a practice. Drawing the breath. There were 5 ideas but now what is it? Then I must be in action...

I understand it so well; this feeling of being not there today. Out. Out. Out. Out. Wow, what an idea to write close to the assemblage of guests and staff. So hard to concentrate.

Why did i want to come closer? Get in touch. Not feel separated. Whatever the reasons were, they pull me out of the focus, the task becomes blurry. J's music is all over me. So present. Is that how it feels, when Oracle is around, while other people try to focus on something else? An external source of sound. Information Information that you might not want to process in this moment.

H is having fun with the nurse-stagiaires. But with who doesn't he have fun? A very talented young man, when it comes to social situations.

"Je bent een petit chat."

A special moment outside. A place not quiet, not silent, but not noisy neither. The nature plays with its possibilities of sound, the airplane 'noise' above us and our vocals join this orchestra.

Somehow this moment embraces us well enough, so we could go deep into the practice. Hanging on a branch, my body was reacting to the waves of the wind, the voice stays reactive to it as well. The whole body listens; not just to the sounds, but to all impulses and elements. H couldn't stand still, while he was doing his practice. Maybe his body reacted as well to the overflow of information.

How an isolated place can still be so full of information. I was so impressed with his voice, his range and possibilities, his dedication to the moment. He dived totally into it. It touched me to watch and listen. At one point he sounded like a crier, my mind directly went to M. I wonder how she is doing. R-M is in a very good mood today, while R fell down the stairs. So many different emotions, so many different states of being and still everyone is together.

R is in a lot of pain. I chose without knowing it to score her breath. Now i feel like a voyeur to score her while she is in pain. How did this choice happen? I didn't know....

Beginning slowly going with my energy or lack of it. My experiment of going with my lack of energy. This is a weird feeling. I still functioned but at a lower level a reclusive approach but we still managed to have a great day. So this is good news to me that I can come here and come with what I have. I mean what is the choice? I think if I feel like this then normally I force myself to rise up against it. Maybe it's the huge piece of meat that my body is dealing with. Big lot of meat last night and today. So much animal. And what is today? I feel empty. I feel settled in. There is crazy energy. Yelling, laughing, a fire drill. And only 10 guests. Almost the same amount of workers to guests. Who else is going to play?

NB: Bring portable vinyl player for J.

27 November 2018

calmness. covered in calmness. Nowhere, but still somewhere. Where is somewhere? The radio plays, J is playing the radio, the others are playing with Rummy stones, someone is knitting, we are doing what we usually do. The WALL. THE WALL. There's a wall. What wall am i talking about. Maybe an invisible wall inside of me. A lack of understanding. There is always a lack of understanding. Who thinks he knows, goes nowhere, but up his own asshole. Deep down into his own shit. Continue. Just keep on walking. Getting lost. But you are already lost. Can i get lost-er? Who of us is the lost-est? We are lost in each other. Trying to find ourselves in each other- or trying to find each other in ourselves. M is searching for contact. Lost-er seems not a bad place to be.

L o s t n e s s .

Concreteness. Making things clear? Not necessary. Do we know what we are doing? and why? I don't know why we are here, but I do know I feel right at this very moment a warm feeling inside me at the zone of the chest. A softening of the muscles. Perhaps it is from J's vocals & touch. We had just done an exercise of listening to the inside, allowing voice to travel to places of the body that is touched by the other person. Somehow I feel I can focus on myself, my feelings & interior while still being aware of what's around me. H & B chatting & trying to get our attention. I can still stay with myself.

https://soundcloud.com/user-526820289/publication

Illustrations: scores by Oracle,
collectively drawn with Hicham

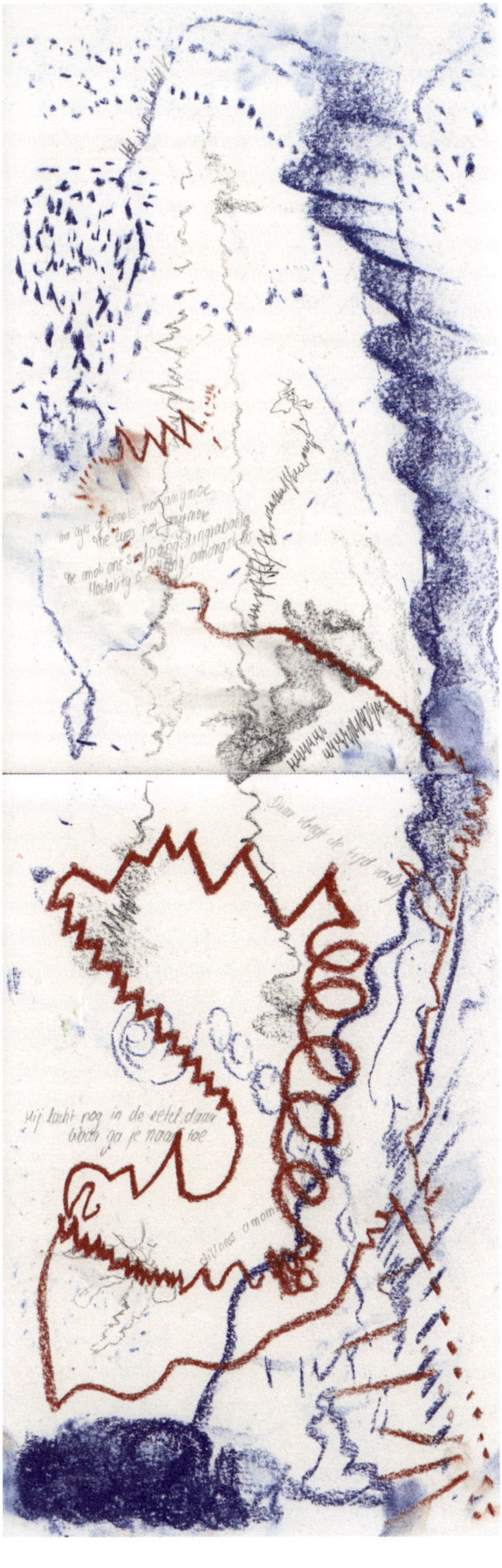
Hij lacht nog in de wereld daar
Waar ga je naar toe

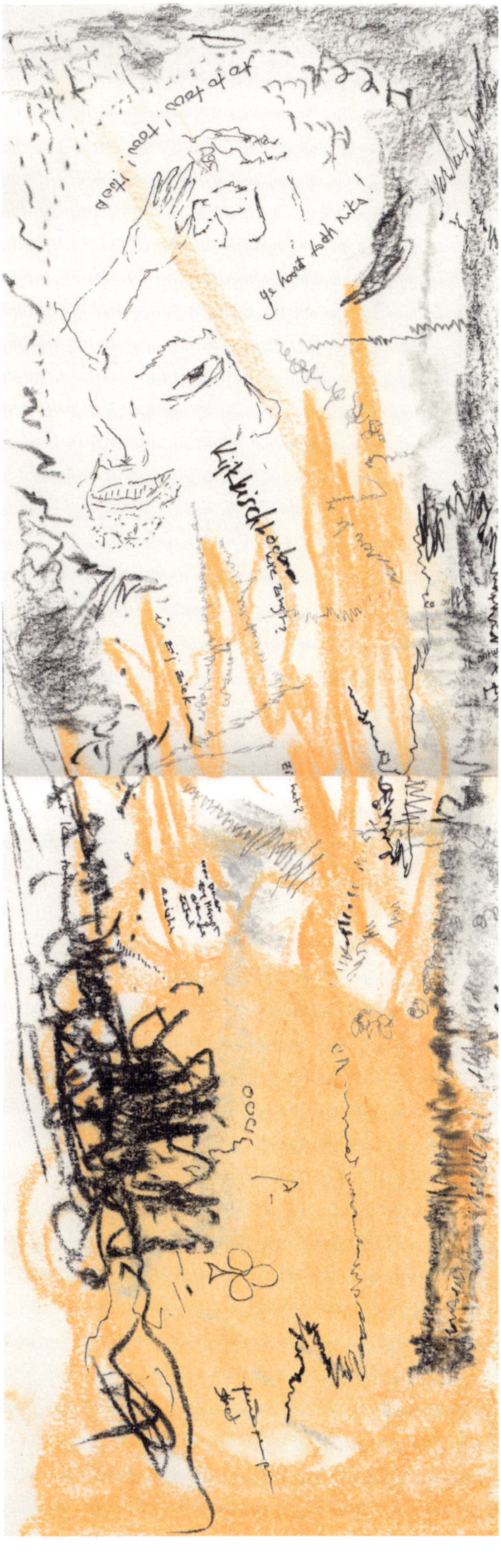

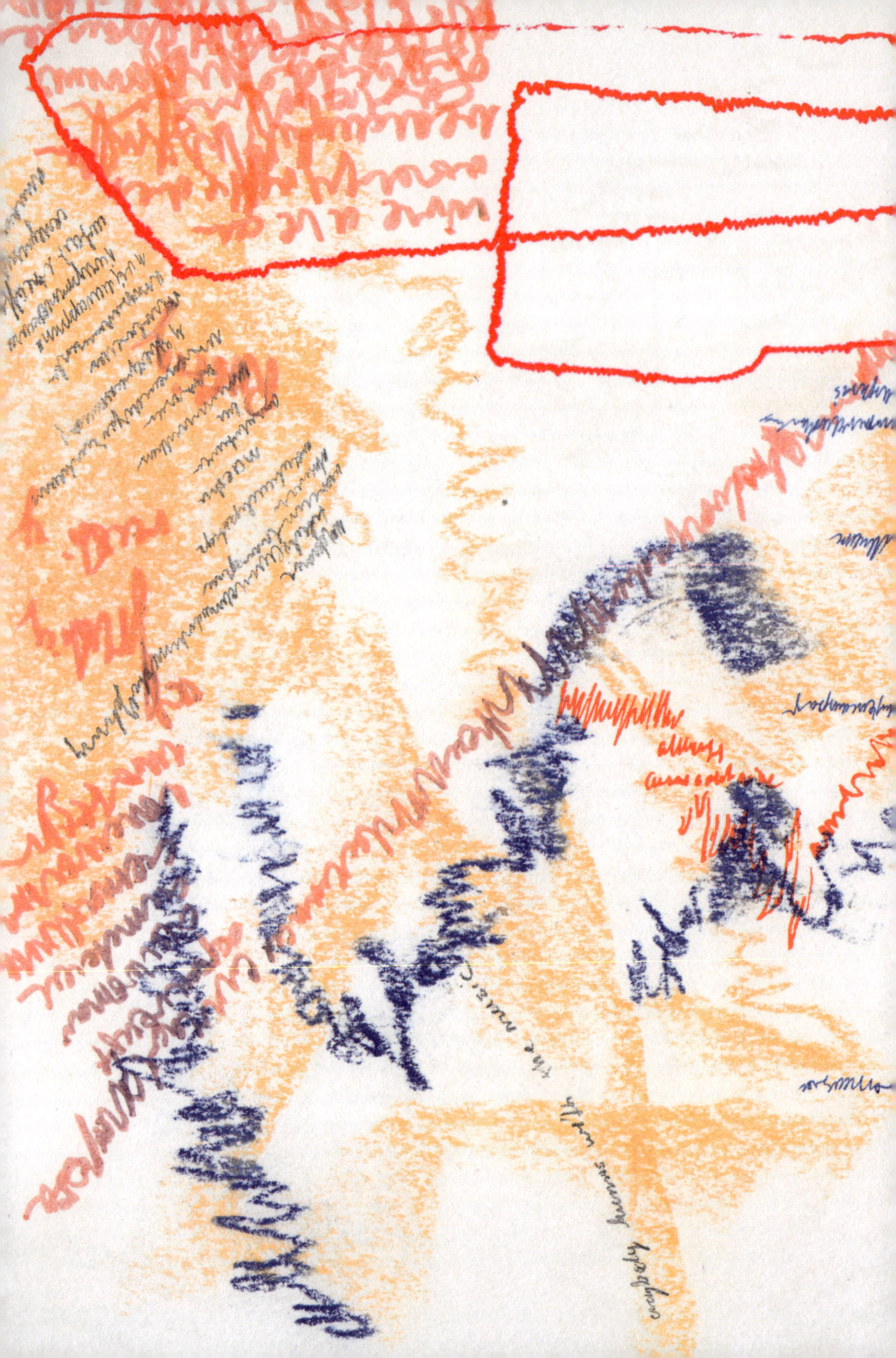
everybody becomes with the music

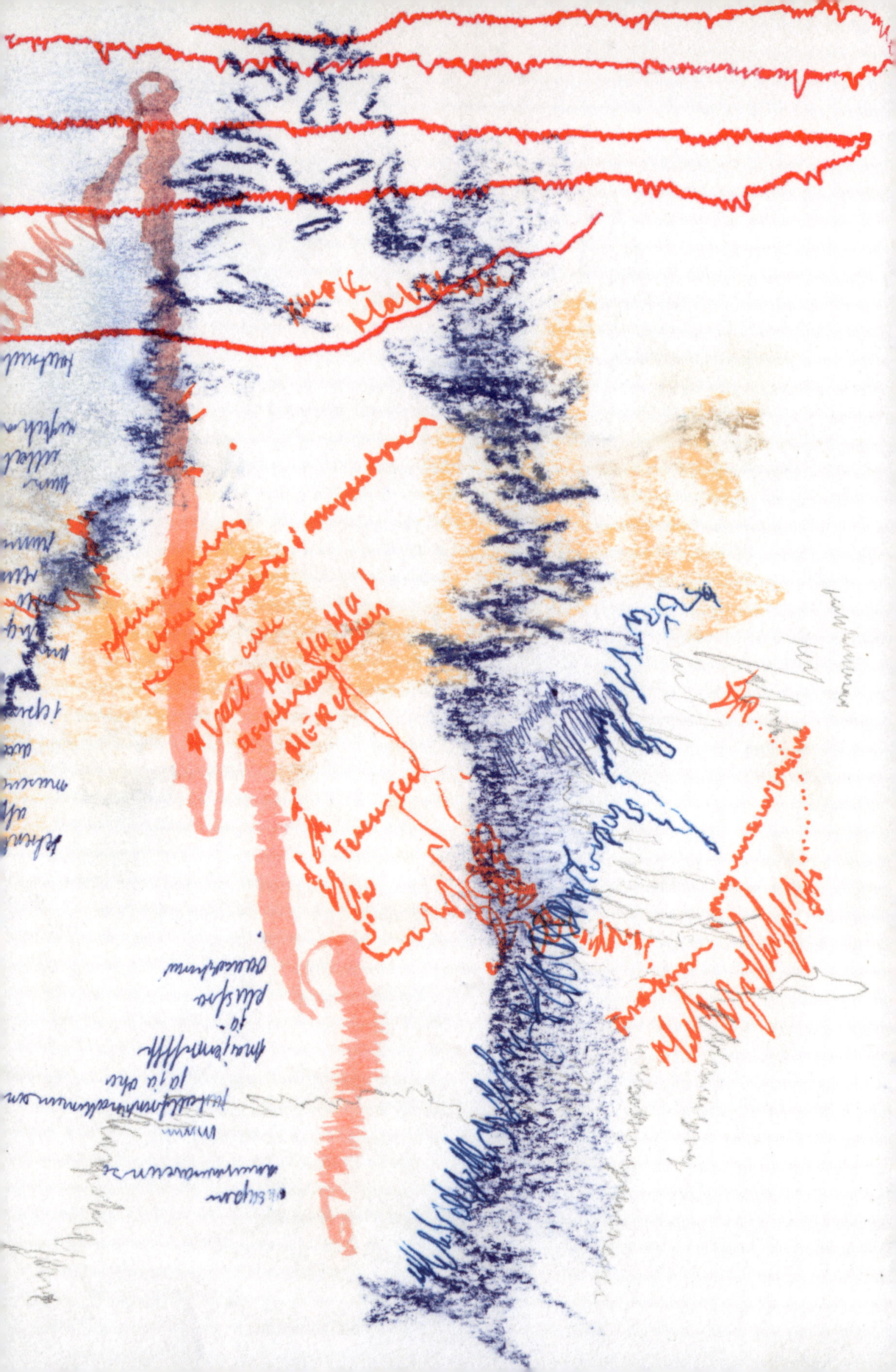

152

THE BEAUTIFULLY SIMPLE

153

Some people seem to ascribe almost miraculous and transcendental powers to art. While no one doubts that art can indeed have incredible effects, according to artists, their work is often first and foremost a 'practice': an extension, a crystallisation or a catalyst of life. Monumental projects can catch the eye, but small, down-to-earth artistic gestures can also provide inspiration, wonder or connection and bring comfort or joy. Making a statement doesn't have to be done loudly; it can also be achieved through the small, the quiet, the inward-looking or the beautifully simple. This is what writer Rudi Meulemans observed, as an outside eye, in the project IN/FINITY. His reflections and writings resulted in a literary triptych, depicting precious moments when art meets life—and death—during the IN/FINITY project, but also in the work of various writers and artists that inspire him. Meulemans also fondly remembers artists who died during the AIDS crisis, a trauma that the art world, hit hard by AIDS, suppressed for a long time.

The sea, the sea
Rudi Meulemans

1.

Last year I was standing on Long Island, looking out at the sea. I couldn't imagine what was on the other side. There had to be something across the water. But what?

When I look at the sea here in Ostend, I know that England is out there, somewhere in the distance. On the other side of the North Sea lies Dungeness, the place where Derek Jarman once lived. We once had great plans. But Derek was sick. AIDS. He would die a year after I met him.

Derek had a number of cult films to his name, but for his last project, which was based on a novel by James Purdy, he couldn't secure the financing. No insurance company wanted to take on the risk, since he was incurably ill.

But Derek didn't give up. He always used to say: 'If I don't have money for 35 mm, I'll shoot on 8 mm.' Blue, his last movie, is a testament to that tenacity. Derek was all but blind. From inside the hospital, he made a movie consisting of a blue screen and an audio track largely recorded in his room, at his bedside.

There, across the sea, in Dungeness, we celebrated his last birthday. Several months earlier, I had been present when he consecrated the marriage between two women at the tide line. It was an alternative ceremony, because same-sex marriage was not yet legal in England. Doing what you want to do. That was what it was all about. Letting neither laws nor illness stand in the way of your dreams. A marriage by the sea, a vow 'until death do us part'.

2.

After the death of his wife, the author and philosopher Iris Murdoch, John Bayley wrote:

I can hardly believe it is all over. [1]

For months, the professor of English literature had cared for his terminally ill wife, who was suffering from Alzheimer's. When she could no longer write, he took over. The back cover of his book shows a picture of the couple by the sea. Iris looks out across the water. Her eyes are dull. John stands behind, leaning against her. Her fragile body catches the wind. It looks as if she's supporting him. The sick person protecting the carer.

Bayley writes that Iris suddenly started to deteriorate rapidly in the last three weeks of her life. It became impossible to reach her. It appears that the patient enters a dark space. Perhaps, in this space, they have an own way of knowing, an own way of doing things. The body goes its own way until it disappears.

(...) nothing human is eternal. For us, eternity is like an illusion.

wrote Iris Murdoch in her 1978 Booker Prize-winning novel, 'The Sea, the Sea'. In the opening paragraph, she wielded her pen as William Turner had taken up a brush to evoke the sea.

"With the tide turning, it leans quietly against the land, almost unflecked by ripples or by foam. Near to the horizon it is a luxurious purple, spotted with regular lines of emerald green. At the horizon it is indigo. Near to the shore, where my view is framed by rising heaps of humpy yellow rock, there is a band of lighter green, icy and pure, less radiant, opaque however, not transparent."

3.

This description beautifully fits a small painting by Bruno Van Dijck which hangs in my study.

Over there, across the water, the painter seeks out desolate places along the British coast for his pictorial practice. He focuses on the shorelines. During his fieldwork, he paints the same coastal landscape twenty-four, thirty-six, even forty-eight times on small wooden panels.

Over time this landscape, to which he devotes his careful attention, will disappear under the influence of climate change. We will lose this image of the sea. This is why the panels are kept in a case placed on a matching plinth, as a relic shrine. This ritual aspect of the work is of the utmost importance. The pictorial practice as a mourning process: the artist mourns that which passes. Nothing lasts forever. Not even the sea.

[1] John Bayley, *Iris. A memoir of Iris Murdoch,* London: Duckworth, 1998

Lest we perish
Personal notes on IN/FINITY
Rudi Meulemans

"Dying is terrible. There's no consolation in it at all.

Therefore, we construct art, and we construct religion, we construct a lot of our institutions as ways of dealing with death."

— Stephen Jay Gould

*

1993. A few weeks until Christmas.

My friend and I are driving to Zaventem airport to pick up British filmmaker Derek Jarman. For over a year now, I've been working on a stage adaptation of Derek's diaries. In Modern Nature, Derek talks about his last years, about the way he deals with the illness. Derek had AIDS.

As he comes through the security check he's leaning on Keith, his partner, whom he always called HB. It's short for Hinney Beast, a nickname from Newcastle, Keith's hometown.

Derek is nearly blind. I stroke his shoulder, his arm. Then he smiles.

'I can almost see you.'

We get in the car and drive toward the theatre in the centre of the city. On the way, it starts to snow.

'Look Derek, look, it's snowing,' HB says.

'How wonderful. I thought I would never see snow again.'

*

Wemmel, Thursday March 2, 2017.

TOPAZ, the VUB's day care centre for supportive and palliative care. It's someone's birthday. The volunteers take the bottles of cava out of the fridge. Someone heats up the quiches. The guests are gathered in the living room. We raise our glasses.

Then Jorge arrives. They've

reserved a conference room for him to work in. Two of the guests, Houssine and Molla, are eager to get started. A few others are curious and come along to watch.

Jorge demarcates an area within the room. This is the stage. He's not looking at this stage as a dramaturge, but as a visual artist. To him, the stage is a plane, a canvas on which to place objects. In this environment, bodies become artworks in an exhibition space.

It begins with a blank canvas. Houssine starts placing objects on it. A cloth, a chair, bandages, a plastic container with water, a pair of scissors, blue vinyl gloves. Then Molla enters the space. He takes off his cap, puts it on the chair. He takes off his track jacket. Then he lies down on the cloth on the floor. He shows Houssine his left arm. Houssine kneels down beside him. The ritual begins. Covering the arm with plaster. The two men communicate through looks. Once the arm is completely wrapped up, Houssine leaves the room. Molla stays behind, alone. He looks at his wrapped-up arm. It will take time for the plaster to dry. Here, it's not about the outcome, but about the act of creation. Actions are performed as time passes.

⋆

In a small valley in the Peloponnese, in Epidaurus, you can visit the remains of the Temple of Asclepius. Only a few stones remain of the building that stood here in the fourth century BC. But in what was once the cella, a depression in the floor still shows where the cult statue once stood.

A place to come for those who had fallen ill.

A place to participate in a ritual.

In a separate room in the sanctuary, the sick person was cleansed. An animal was sacrificed and the sick person was wrapped up in the skin stripped from the animal. Then, the sick person would go to sleep in the Abaton.

At night, Asclepius would appear in the shape of a dog, announcing healing. Even if, upon awakening, the sick person had not really been healed, the dream would still bring him consolation.

⋆

Brussels, Wednesday, April 19, 2017

A dance studio at P.A.R.T.S. Vera has invited a string quartet. They play Haydn. The guests from Topaz who are in attendance have never before sat down to listen to classical music. For a moment, it feels as though we've entered a different world. A different time, where mortality no longer applies. I forget the hundred-and-one things I still have to do later. I dissolve into the music.

Then the musicians stop playing. They lay their instruments aside. Now, we take the place of the instruments. One of the guests becomes the viola, another the cello, yet another the second violin. I give the violinist my arm. We listen to a recording of the same Haydn string quartet. The musicians play our body parts. The violinist's fingers lightly tap my arm. A choreography for violinists' fingers. I see the others absorbed in the moment.

Afterwards, I wonder what it was that made this afternoon

important to the guests. The rehearsal room is a safe space. The atmosphere is calm, everyone cares for one another. Nothing can happen. The artists are there for the guests, and vice versa. For the guests, was this afternoon about the music, or about the art? Or was it about the attention they received? And what about the artists?

*

February 2004.

My father is lying on a bed in the emergency room of the university hospital of Leuven. He's probably naked. A white sheet covers him. But his bare feet are sticking out at the end. I keep looking at those feet the entire time.

Before they wheel him off to the operating room, he says: 'Take good care of your mother.'

A few days later, he dies. And all I keep thinking is: 'What can I do for her?'

One evening, I'm sitting in her living room. I put on a CD. Bach's Cello Suites. We listen. After a while, my mother asks me to turn off the music. Now we sit together in silence. She takes my hand in hers.

*

After the rehearsal of Modern Nature, HB and I walk with Derek through the Saint-Hubert Royal Galleries. Derek would like to go to a restaurant. Even though he himself barely eats anything these days.

Derek walks in between us. HB and I support him on either side. He's breathing heavily. Halfway down the gallery, he loses his trousers, which fall down to his ankles.

'Oh dear.'

He's become so terribly thin.

HB says: 'You can still become a clown, Derek. Entertain the people. You've got the talent to become a clown.'

*

Some believe that art, great art, should unsettle. Goya's 'Los desastres de la Guerra'. Andres Serrano's 'Piss Christ'. Or Damien Hirst's 'The Physical Impossibility of Death in the Mind of Someone Living'.

Others believe that art should console. A still life by Jan Davidszoon de Heem. Henri Matisse's 'La Chapelle du Rosaire'. Or a swimming pool by David Hockney.

On a London wall, Banksy sprays the words: 'Art should comfort the disturbed and disturb the comfortable.'

In the first place, of course, art doesn't have to do anything.

*

In a note in his diary, Derek writes how, after his doctor has given him the diagnosis, he walks home from the hospital. On the way, he sees a pair of shoes in a window display. Beautiful shoes. He wants to go in to try them on, maybe buy them. But then he thinks: Do I still need a new pair of shoes?

*

"The arts aid the personality in its struggle with ambivalence and helplessness, because they nourish the capacity to experience joy in human finitude."

— Martha Nussbaum

*

Friday, August 18, 2017. After lunch at TOPAZ, Emi draws aside with one of the guests. She has invited an illustrator to join them with his sketchbook that afternoon. Emi asks the guest where he would still want to travel. The guest is from Ethiopia, and tells her he dreams of traveling to its highest mountain, the Ras Dashan, at the source of the Blue Nile. He has never been there, but he knows what the mountain and its trails look like. He describes how he would pitch a tent, build a bonfire, sit and watch night fall. The illustrator draws what the guest describes. 'Yes,' the guest says, 'that's it. That's exactly it.' He tells us about the animals in the mountains, the gelada baboon and the Ethiopian walia ibex. Emi looks up pictures of these animals on her iPhone. The illustrator draws them in the landscape. The guest looks at the drawing. 'Yes,' he says, 'that's where I want to go.'

*

March 16, 2017.

Early Thursday afternoon in the day care centre. A few guests and volunteers are sitting on chairs gathered in a circle. Michael is teaching breathing exercises. We have to inhale deeply and then exhale audibly. A long breath, eyes closed. I try. I join in. My head starts to swim. Then I hear the breathing of the others. The sound of breath. With my eyes closed, I see a room in the intensive care unit. My father is hooked up to a ventilator. I hear the sound of the machine. Mechanical breathing. And later, after the machine has been turned off, nothing.

*

"We possess art lest we perish of the truth."

— Friedrich Nietzsche

*

Late January, 1994.

Derek had been admitted to the hospital. But on his birthday, January 31st, he insisted on being taken to his cottage on the coast of Dungeness. We had gathered there with a few friends. We sat Derek in a comfortable chair by the window. Outside, we'd built a large bonfire. In the distance, you could see the sparkling lights of the nuclear plant. HB lit fireworks. All Derek could still see was a few sparkles. Tilda Swinton was kneeling next to him, describing everything there was to see. After a while, Derek became too tired. He asked them to take him back. Back to the hospital. That night in the hospital, he wrote his very last words in his diary:

Birthday.
Fireworks.
HB true love.

1.

In the month of May, when Mary is honoured, my mother unfailingly makes her pilgrimage to Scherpenheuvel, where the Virgin Mother has been the focal point of popular devotion since the fourteenth century. In 1304, Lodewijk van Velthem, then chaplain in Scherpenheuvel-Zichem, spoke in his book 'Spieghel Historiael' of a wondrous oak tree, which had grown in the shape of a cross. A statue of the Virgin Mary was hung on the tree, drawing believers from all around the area. Even when the statue disappeared during the turbulent years of the Reformation, the pilgrims kept coming. At the end of the sixteenth century, a new statue was hung on the tree: Our Lady of Scherpenheuvel. In time, a small chapel was erected near the oak tree, and the renown of the place spread across the whole of Europe.

The pilgrimage of archdukes Albrecht and Isabella to Scherpenheuvel in 1603, to give thanks for the Spanish troops' victory over the protestants at 's Hertogenbosch, was a highlight in the history of the devotion. They were so impressed by the place that, six years later, they themselves came to lay the first stone of the baroque church built here, which would receive the title of basilica in 1922. The church designed by Wenceslas Coeberger is laid out in the shape of a seven-pointed star, symbolising the seven joys and seven sorrows of Mary.

The Caravaggist Theodoor van Loon was asked to create seven works about the life of Mary. The architect and the painter had already worked together on the Chapel of St. Hubert at Albrecht and Isabella's hunting lodge in Tervuren. Van Loon created enormous paintings, one for each of the six side chapels, and an assumption piece for the main altar, in the same place where the miraculous oak once stood.

As a young girl, my mother and her friends would ride their bikes from Grobbendonk to Scherpenheuvel. It was a journey of roughly thirty-five kilometres. On arrival, they would join others at long wooden tables, drink coffee poured from large pots and eat the sandwiches they had brought from home. Then it was time for Mass in the basilica, and the Stations of the Cross on the surrounding hill. Before starting on her journey back home, my mother would buy a fanion with an image of the Madonna and attach it to the luggage rack on the back of her bicycle. All the way home, she and her friends would sing songs in praise of the Holy Virgin.

Her whole life, my mother has continued to visit Scherpenheuvel every year in the month of May. She used to drive there with my father, and now she is widowed her friends come to pick her up. She no longer buys fanions for her bicycle. But she always searches one of the remaining souvenir booths for white candles with an image of Our Lady of Scherpenheuvel. At home, she lights these candles in what she calls 'the chapel of the heath'. The registry of architectural heritage officially lists it as the 'Chapel of Our Lady of the Immaculate Conception', but some call it the 'Chapel of Our Lady of Lourdes' because of the smaller-scale replica of the Lourdes grotto constructed inside. This is the local translation of something larger.

As with most of these centres of

popular devotion, it was not commissioned by the official church. It was Mrs. Medard Dieltjes, a trader in building materials, who commissioned the place of worship in 1911.

From the outside, it looks like a church in miniature. It is comprised of a nave with a single bay under a gable roof and a turret-shaped east choir under a tent roof. The roofs are made of artificial slate over bordering brick friezes. Both the nave and choir have round-arched openings in the wall.

The interior is plastered and painted sky blue. In the Lourdes grotto, behind an iron fence which was crafted by the local blacksmith, stands a statue of Our Lady. The statue was purchased by Mrs. Dieltjens in Liège along with the Stations of the Cross, a set of small watercolour paintings, of which the third station was stolen. Around the head of Mary sits a metal wreath with the words:

'I AM THE IMMACULATE CONCEPTION'.

Until this very day, the neighbours maintain the chapel. This is where people from the village come to pray when one of their loved ones falls ill. They ask Mary for recovery. When one of their loved one passes away, they seek consolation with her. This is where my mother comes now that my father is no longer with us.

2.

In 1941, the doctors had given up Henri Matisse. He was suffering from throat cancer and had already been operated. And yet, despite the surgeon's bleak prognosis, the artist was to leave the hospital in an almost miraculous way three months later. Matisse was then seventy-two years old, and was to live for another thirteen years. These were his 'stolen years', during which he was particularly creative, flouted all the rules and did only what he wanted to do. He himself referred to this period as 'une seconde vie'.

During his recovery, he was attended by a young night nurse, Monique Bourgeois. They developed a friendship and she became his model for various drawings and a number of paintings.

Later on Monique struggles with her own health and goes to live with the Dominican Sisters in Vence. Matisse lives directly opposite the convent in the villa Le Rêve. A year later, Monique decides to enter the convent, taking the name Sister Jacques-Marie. The friendship between the artist and the nun continues: they carry on an extensive correspondence. When Matisse visits her in the convent and sees her in her habit for the first time, he is deeply moved.

At the time, the Dominican Sisters don't have a chapel worthy of the name. Their prayer services are held in an old garage with a leaking roof. When Sister Jacques-Marie tells Matisse they have building plans, he proposes to design the chapel. He is to work on this project continuously for the next four years.

High over Nice, along a bend in

the road in the town of Vence, lies the slightly hidden Chapelle du Rosaire. Atop its blue roof, as a beacon and only sign of the building's religious purpose, sits a thirteen metres tall wrought iron cross, with golden crescents and flames at its ends. On the street side, nothing else can be seen except a blind whitewashed wall and a small door.

Inside, you find yourself in the harmonious chapel for which Matisse designed everything down to the smallest detail: the blue and yellow glass windows, the white tiles with black figures, the altar, the small cross and even the chasubles worn by the priests during the worship service.

In 1908, Matisse wrote in his Notes d'un peintre that he dreamed of a serene art, an art to calm and soothe the spirit. This is what he achieved here, in the Chapelle du Rosaire, and this is why it is indeed, as he himself considered it to be, his masterpiece.

It was Sister Jacques-Marie who showed him the way to this Gesamtkunstwerk. She passed away in 2005, and was given a funeral service in the chapel. On her casket lay a bunch of anemones, Matisse's favourite flower.

3.

On top of the Colline de Boulémont near Ronchamp, in the nature park of the Ballons des Vosges in the French region Bourgogne-Franche-Comté, stands the pilgrimage chapel Notre Dame du Haut, designed by Le Corbusier.

Like Henri Matisse, Le Corbusier was not religious. Both had been sought out by the Dominican Marie-Alain Couturier, who was looking to engage the best artists for the church as part of the Art Sacré movement in the middle of the last century. He believed that a masterpiece crafted by an unbeliever would always be more effective than work of lesser quality created by a believer. When he asked the sculptor Jacques Lipchitz to create a sculpture of the Virgin Mother for Notre Dame de Toute Grâce du Plateau d'Assy, the latter had asked him: 'But don't you know I'm a Jew?' To which Couturier responded: 'If it doesn't bother you, it won't bother me either'.

The pilgrimage chapel of Ronchamp goes back to Celtic times. The name Notre Dame du Haut dates from the eighteenth century. In 1924, a lightning strike destroyed the sanctuary. This was replaced by a neo-Gothic building, which was bombed at the end of the Second World War. For the reconstruction of the chapel, Father Couturier invited Le Corbusier to visit the site. After some hesitation, Le Corbusier travelled to Ronchamp. Standing on the hill, he looked across the wide panorama, the horizon all around him.

The chapel Le Corbusier sketched carried on the shapes of this rolling landscape. The neighbouring

Vosges mountains inspired the concave shapes, its valleys the convex forms. The architecture is an answer to the surrounding nature.

When I climb the hill from the new visitors' centre, designed by Renzo Piano, the first thing I see is the enormous concrete shell that forms the roof of the chapel. Next, I see the tall white tower of the south-eastern chapel, and only then do I see the white wall with its irregular openings. I've arrived here, quite by accident, on September 8th, the day of the Nativity of Mary. For the occasion, which draws numerous pilgrims to the chapel, the monumental door decorated with coloured enamel is wide open. That unchangeable enamel underlines the power of the rough concrete construction, exposed to the elements. On all other days of the year, you have to walk all the way around the building to enter through a smaller wooden door. But today, I enter by the front door.

The chapel is half-dark. The light coming in from the top of the south-eastern chapel is touching. At the other end of the chapel, the benches are grouped together on a platform, leaving the rest of the space empty. In front of the stage is a large candleholder with slender, white candles. Remarkably, the roof is not supported either by the southern or by the eastern wall. A thin strip of light runs between the roof and the walls. A niche, open on two sides, high over the altar, houses a seventeenth-century polychrome statue of Mary with Child.

4.

As part of a project to bring therapy and art closer together, the Psychiatric Centre of Duffel commissioned Thierry de Cordier to build a chapel. The choice of this artist was not arbitrary. In his work, de Cordier frequently seeks out the world's sanctuaries. In collaboration with Patrick Lefebure of Archipel Architects, he designed an empty space symbolising complete rest. It became a quiet room for patients and visitors to retreat in.

The proportions were determined by the golden ratio. The structure consists of a tall black box (12.5 meters in length, 5.5 meters in width and 5.5 meters in height). On the outside, a double layer of roofing was applied and coated with pitch. Through an opening in the roof, a freestanding white wall, eight metres tall, protrudes.

Inside the space, opposite this wall, there is a concrete bench for visitors to sit on. Through the gap in the roof, the visitor can see the surrounding nature, the green foliage of trees. The sun shining in creates a streak of light on the side wall. The side walls are weathered. Only the tall wall is painted white every year. This wall, which de Cordier called 'the wall of nothing', reminds me of a film screen on which you can project your thoughts.

While I'm sitting here, absorbing the effects of the room, a young girl comes in. She looks sad. She sits down next to me on the concrete bench. Her fingernails are painted in Marian blue. This is the 'Chapel of nothing'.

165

166

167

BREATH OF LIFE

169

Our breath is considered the source of life, while at the same time, the end of breathing symbolises the end of that life. It drives one of our most human features: the voice, our ability to speak and sing. In various forms of art, breath plays a more prominent role than we would expect (for instance, in dance, theatre and music). Many illnesses also have a direct impact on our breathing, ranging from a simple cold to more severe symptoms such as the failure of speech, difficulty breathing or a change of voice. Art and health projects using breath or voice often turn out to be highly confronting for the participants. Such projects confront limits and often also push those limits. They render them irrelevant or even reveal the poetry in them.

With his 'BREATHCORE', Michael Schmid explores modes of collectivity through the practice of breathing. Instead of looking at breath from an individual health viewpoint, each person's breath becomes part of a collective resonance.

BREATHCORE
Michael Schmid

The project BREATHCORE has been an ongoing investigation of the dynamics of breath within a social, artistic and political context.

Michael Schmid initiated the project in the summer of 2015 and has ever since organized a number of BREATHCORES for different cultural venues and festivals with over 300 active participants.

In 2017, Michael Schmid developed 'BREATHCORE—the score' together with the guests of TOPAZ during his residency at IN/FINITY. The focus lay on the development of a breathing score for a public.

In this publication you find a set of breathing instructions, which, when executed correctly, will evoke certain mental, emotional, sensational and physical states. This serves the unfolding of a silent, inner dramaturgy for the participating readers who will modify their perception through breathing.

'BREATHCORE—the score' can be performed by anyone. Breath is generic and a tool shared by all humans. The instructions are simple and easy to follow. The presented scores have different inspirations: Some have been newly conceived, others have been inspired by literature of various cultures and sources —copied, combined or modified.

BREATHCORE THE SCORE
EIGHT WAYS TO EXPERIENCE INFINITY

The **SCORES** are conceived for successive performance.

Follow the **INSTRUCTIONS** as precisely as possible:

READ the complete page **CAREFULLY** before performing a **SCORE.** (Detail in execution will make a major difference!)

SIT UPRIGHT on a chair or on the ground (in **EASY POSE**) with a straight spine unless otherwise indicated.

Don't **FORCE**—in case you get dizzy, **REDUCE** the intensity or **STOP.**

Be **PHYSICAL** if necessary. Make **NOISE** at times. **LISTEN.** Use your **BODY.** Have **FUN!**

OBSERVE how your perception changes with each score.

Use a **TIMER** for the indicated durations.

total duration: ± 45 minutes

BEFORE

CLOSE your **EYES.** **BREATHE** smoothly through your **NOSE.** **RELAX** every muscle.

LISTEN to the **SOUND** of your **BREATH** —its tone, rhythm, speed, and smoothness / harshness.

FEEL the breath through the **EXPANSION** and **CONTRACTION** of your body.

FEEL the **BREATH** going through your nostrils, down your throat, into your lungs and back up.

VISUALIZE an imaginary **CIRCLE** **INFLATING** and **DEFLATING** at the **RHYTHM** of your **RESPIRATION**

duration 3 minutes
(use your TIMER)

NOW

STAND like a **SUMO** wrestler. (Legs slightly spread, hands on your knees supporting your upper body.)

Take a **FULL BREATH** through your **MOUTH.**

EXHALE immediately and quickly take another deep breath.

Breathe deeply **IN-OUT IN-OUT** etc. as vigorously as possible. (As if panting for breath after having run a fast kilometer.)

If you feel **TENSION** or **DIZZINESS** breathe more **GENTLY.**

Do 10 **INHALES** and 10 **EXHALES.**

RESUME to **NORMAL** breathing, take a moment to stretch your entire body in all possible directions.

REPEAT 3 times

Take a **FULL BREATH** in
through your **NOSE.**

EXHALE through your **MOUTH**
as **GENTLY** and **SMOOTHLY**
as possible
for at least 30 **SECONDS.**

Imagine **SILENTLY** fogging
a **M I R R O R .**

Your breath is a **BRIDGE** between
your **INTERIOR** and your **EXTERIOR.**

MINIMIZE the exhalation
to **AMPLIFY** the impact.

RESUME to **NORMAL** breathing.

REPEAT 3 times

ABSOLUTE

INHALE through your **NOSE**
TAKE the **AIR IN** exactly
from the back of the
B E L L Y B U T T O N .

PUSH the **AIR** strongly
UP and **FORWARD**
until it reaches the back of the
SHOULDER BONES.

HOLD it firmly and
COMPRESS it all over the
BACK SIDE.

GENTLY EXHALE & REPEAT

duration 3 minutes
(use your TIMER)

BREATHE through your **NOSE.**

INHALE while counting 4 **BEATS** (± 4 seconds)
HOLD your **BREATH** for 8 **BEATS.**
EXHALE for 16 **BEATS.**
HOLD on **EMPTY** for 4 **BEATS.**

IMMEDIATELY REPEAT the process without resuming to normal breathing.

When breathing IN imagine inhaling goodness, light, and energy. When breathing OUT, imagine exhaling tensions, illness, anger and fear.

REPEAT for 7 MINUTES
(use your TIMER)

INHALE DEEPLY by the **NOSE,**
EXHALE DEEPLY by the **MOUTH.**

When **EXHALING** imagine fogging a **MIRROR** like a sonorous **WHISPER**
(" ... H A A A A A A A A ... ")

Even out any irregularities your breath might have.

LISTEN to the **RESONANCE** of your **BREATH** creating the **SOUND** of the **OCEAN.**

SURF on your **BREATH** and **ALLOW** your **BODY** to **VIBRATE.**

REPEAT for 5 minutes
(use your TIMER)

DRINK a glass of **WATER.**

Sit with a **STRAIGHT SPINE.**
PLACE your arms across your chest
LOCK the **HANDS** under the **ARMPITS**
with the **PALMS OPEN**
and against the **BODY.**

RAISE your **SHOULDERS**
up towards your **EARS**
and bring your **CHIN** to your **CHEST.**

BREATHE through your **NOSE.**
CLOSE your **EYES.**

INHALE	7	seconds
HOLD	7	seconds
EXHALE	6	seconds

REPEAT for 3 to 11 minutes
(use your TIMER)

INMOST

Take 3 full breaths **IN** through your **NOSE** and **OUT** through your **MOUTH.**
EXHALE fully.
PAUSE shortly.

WITHOUT INHALING any air **EXHALE AGAIN,** pushing out more remaining air.

RELEASE any **TENSION.**

EXHALE a last time, **EMPTYING** your lungs **COMPLETELY.**

HOLD your **BREATH** for as **LONG** as **POSSIBLE** without forcing.
PUSH your limits **GENTLY!**

REPEAT 3 times

INFINITE

Sit with a **STRAIGHT SPINE.**

Bring your **HANDS** together in front of your **CHEST** without touching it.

Touch the **TIPS** of your **THUMBS** and the **TIPS** of your **PINKIES.** The remaining three fingers point up like **ANTANNAE** with a **SPACE** in-between the **PALMS.**

Look at the tip of your **NOSE.**

PUCKER your **LIPS** and **INHALE** through the **MOUTH.**

Powerfully **EXHALE** through the **NOSE** using the **NAVAL POINT** to push all the **AIR OUT.**

to **FINISH:**

INHALE, HOLD briefly, and **RELAX.**

REPEAT for 11 minutes
(use your TIMER)

181

Colophon & Credits

Chief Editors:
Wouter Bouchez & Julie Rodeyns

Final Editor/Translator:
Free De Backer & Leah Wolfe

Graphic Design:
6'56"

Authors/Contributors/Images:
Christian Bakalov, Hilde Bouchez, Wouter Bouchez, Lewis Campbell, Isabelle De Baets, Wim Distelmans, Michael Duckett, Anna Ledgard, Erika Fischer Lichte, Naomi Kerkhove, Emi Kodama, MADLOVE (The Vacuum Cleaner/Hannah Hull), Paul McGee, Rudi Meulemans, Jan Michiels, Oracle (Caroline Daish, Justine Maxelon, Michel Yang), Jérôme Poggi, JS Rafaeli, Julie Rodeyns, Michael Schmid, Vera Tussing, Erik Thys, Ann Weckx.

Thank you:

To all IN/FINITY artists, artistic collaborators and (ex) staff members of TOPAZ and IN/FINITY:
Christian Bakalov, Sabien Bauwens, Wouter Bouchez, Peter Bruynseels, Veva Corthals, Caroline Daish, Inge De Hertogh, Magrit De Maegd, Wim Distelmans, Elias Heuninck, Seb Kann, Ronald Heuninck, Muriel Hérault, Naomi Kerkhove, Emi Kodama, Jorge León, Thomas Luks, Clara Levy & students of the Royal Conservatory Brussels, Anna Luyten, Justine Maxelon, Rudi Meulemans, François Pauwels, Tatyana Petrova, Julie Rodeyns, Michael Schmid, Frank Schweitser, Vera Tussing, Vicky Van de Velde, Hannie Van den Bilcke, Esse Vanderbruggen, Lieve Vande Putte, Jivan van der Ende, Yanna Van Wesemael, Jo Verbiest, Lucie Verbouwe, Ann Weckx, Michel Yang and all the TOPAZ interns.

To the entire volunteer team of TOPAZ, with a special thank you to Hilde Suys for introducing art at TOPAZ for already more than 20 years.

To the people that inspired us leading up to and throughout the project:
Barbara Raes, Delphine Hesters, Dirk De wit, Isabel Vermote, Katleen Van Langendonck, Marianne Van Kerkhoven, Marnix Rummens, Paul De Knop, Ria Van Schoenwinkel, Thérèse Legierse and our entire advisory board.

To the master students:
Nieke Bourgeois, Lissa Camps, Ruth Vermeiren and Laure Verstreken from Vrije Universiteit Brussel and their supervisors Prof. Dr. Free De Backer and Dra. Julie Rodeyns for their critical questions and help along the way.

To our partners:
Kaaitheater, De Markten, Workspace Brussels, Royal Museums of Fine Arts of Belgium, Theater aan Zee, Belgian National Orchestra.

Last but not least:
All our guests

TOPAZ is an initiative of Universitair Ziekenhuis Brussel of Vrije Universiteit Brussel.

TOPAZ
(T)huis voor psychosociale
Oncologie en PAlliatieve Zorg
J. Vander Vekenstraat 158,
1780 Wemmel, Belgium
+32 2 456 82 02
topaz@uzbrussel.be
www.dagcentrum-topaz.be
www.in-finity.be
www.throughartwe.care

This book is a project by:

Created with support of:

184